W9-CEC-078

Prisoners of Hope

Some Books by H. Stuart Hughes

Oswald Spengler: A Critical Estimate
(1952)

The United States and Italy
(1953)

Conciousness and Society:
The Reorientation of European Social Thought 1890–1930
(1958)

History as Art and as Science
(1964)

The Obstructed Path:
French Social Thought in the Years of Desperation 1930–1960
(1968)

The Sea Change: The Migration of Social Thought 1930–1965
(1975)

Prisoners of Hope

The Silver Age of the Italian Jews 1924–1974

H. Stuart Hughes

Harvard University Press
Cambridge, Massachusetts
and London, England
1983

Printed in the United States of America

Library of Congress Cataloging in Publication Data

Hughes, H. Stuart (Henry Stuart), 1916-
Prisoners of hope.

Includes bibliographical references and index.
1. Jews—Italy—Intellectual life.
2. Jews—Italy—History—20th century.
3. Italian literature—Jewish authors—History and criticism.
4. Italy—Ethnic relations.
I. Title.
DS135.I8H83 1983 945'.004924 82-18707
ISBN 0-674-70727-3

To the memory of
Vittorio Calef
1919–1964
poet, diplomat, journalist,
ideological bridgebuilder,
irreplaceable friend

Preface

In writing this book, I have experienced the delight of evoking an *ambiente* with which I feel a profound elective affinity, a sympathy that grew over more than a quarter-century to a point where I found myself impelled to put on paper what up to then had been no more than private reflections. Or perhaps I should date its remote inception back a full half-century, to my first trip to Italy and my first Jewish friendship, and with them the start of a long process of disentanglement from the conventional anti-Semitism which had hedged my childhood.

I cannot possibly list all the Italian friends and aquaintances of Jewish origin whose presence and example, whether in Italy itself or in the congenial atmosphere of the Circolo Italiano di Boston, have inspired my account. Almagià, Contini, Jona, Modigliani, Morpurgo, and Nathan are the family names that spring to mind. I should make special mention of the beginnings of a friendship with Adriano Olivetti, cut short by his untimely death.

I have undertaken in no systematic way to check my findings with the literary protagonists of this study; in the case of living authors such a procedure is potentially embarrassing to both parties. But I should recall several convivial meetings with Carlo Levi in the late 1940s and early 1950s, before I had any idea that I would write about him and his work. I am also grateful for the long and pleasant lunches I enjoyed with Natalia Ginzburg and Giorgio Bassani on a visit to Rome in June 1982, occasions which left me feeling better about certain interpretations of their writings of which I had been far from sure. Neither of course should be held responsible for the result.

At the very start two scholars whom I know only by correspondence kindly helped to orient my still tentative labors: Bernard Dov Cooperman and Magali Sarfatti-Larson. Subsequently, three of my friends and colleagues at the University of California, San Diego—Aaron V. Cicourel, Richard E. Friedman, and Melford E. Spiro—sustained my spirits by indulging (and now and then rectifying) my propensity to hold forth on my favorite topic.

Dante Della Terza, as always, gave generously of his rich literary understanding. Arnaldo Momigliano not only shared with me his unrivaled learning but extended unstinting support at the point in the book's career when I needed it most. Aïda D. Donald, of the Harvard University Press, suggested the title, buoyed my hopes, and got me over the editorial hurdles with her characteristic cheerful efficiency. My wife, Judy, cheered me on, set me right when I was off track, ferreted out inconsistencies in my prose, and maintained my faith in what I was about. Without her confidence in the project I would never have had the courage either to embark on it or to complete it.

H.S.H.

Contents

Prisoners of Hope

1

The Most Ancient of Minorities

What would lead a non-Jew to write of Italian Jewry? What special reason would he have for immersing himself in the twentieth-century vicissitudes of a tiny minority only dimly known beyond Italy's borders?

The reason is quite personal. After a number of years of sustained and close contact with Italy, I suddenly realized that nearly half my Italian acquaintance was of Jewish origin. Up to that time nobody had concealed his Jewish antecedents from me: the matter simply had not come up. When it did so, it was because the information was relevant to something a friend and I were discussing—or possibly it was a sign that we were getting to know each other better. In any case, it was always conveyed matter-of-factly, in a tone neither of boasting nor of apology.

About the same time I began to notice that an inordinately high percentage of Italy's leading contempory writers were similarly of Jewish or part-Jewish origin. Most of these, like my friends, did not stress the fact, and I noticed that biographical sketches of them sometimes did not mention it at all. I knew that the Italian Jews were among the most assimilated in the world and that Italy almost totally lacked a racist or virulently anti-Semitic tradition. What puzzled me, then, was that in such a situation the people whom I knew or whose books I read still identified themselves as Jews and that in most cases this identification still seemed important to them.

In brief, I began to think that a study of the Jewish element in contemporary Italian culture might add something to (or even transcend) the current—and, in our own country, often passionate—debate on assimilation versus Jewish identity. I began to wonder whether it might not be possible *both* to be highly assimilated *and* to treasure one's Jewish heritage. Bit by bit the question formulated itself in my mind: what is left of identity when both language and religion are gone?—a question, incidentally, which could be asked about other minorities in the Western world. And in this wider context, Italian Jewry, as the most ancient minority of any sort, offered the ideal example.

What is more, my Italian experience suggested that the residual sense of Jewishness was a very *private* matter—that is, it was far more perceptible to Italian Jews themselves than to the outsiders who encountered them—a situation just the reverse of the German in 1933. So how was someone like myself to get at it? Here literature again came in as offering the best and possibly the only avenue to understanding. It seemed plausible that even with writers who spoke scarcely at all of their Jewish origins or associations, one might pick up echoes and resonances of a tradition extending back for more than two thousand years.

For me to retrace that history in chronological order would be an unrewarding textbook exercise. Other scholars, versed in Hebrew, as I am not, have already done so.[1] Within the framework of the study I propose, the most pressing initial matter is to account for the tenacity of Italian Judaism. Under some such rubric one may suggest a series of hypotheses, hypotheses which in turn will introduce the minimum of historical and anthropological data requisite for understanding the position of Italian Jews in their country's contemporary culture.

The first thought which springs to mind is that the very longevity and richness of their tradition would prompt in its heirs a particular reluctance to break it off. The oral lore of an ancient ethnic implantation may work as a powerful stimulus to keeping it alive. Just as Rome is the oldest Jewish community in the Western world, so it functions today as by far the largest and most vital such community in all of Italy. And it is here primarily that this century's leading writers of Jewish origin have chosen to live and to work.

According to a common misconception, Italy's Jews have been almost exclusively Sephardic. The statement is correct only in a very loose sense—that is, in the sense that this population has for the most part stemmed from the shores of the Mediterranean and has not spoken Yiddish. In the stricter meaning of Sephardic as deriving from Spain and Portugal, the element in question has ranked for nearly half a millennium as significant but by no means predominant. Iberian Jews did not arrive in Italy in large numbers until the late fifteenth century, and as the fourth in the successive layers of which Italian Jewry was composed.

This notion of layers or accretions fused together over time provides the single most helpful guide to the complexities of a history that has frequently baffled the uninitiated. Schematically (and simplistically) presented, the succession goes about as follows.[2] To an original nucleus of Jews from

Palestine itself—dating back to the Roman Republic and thus already in existence before the massive influx of Jewish slaves in the wake of the Emperor Titus' capture of Jerusalem and destruction of the Temple—there was added in the first millennium of the Christian era a second stratum of merchant families from the Mediterranean diaspora. In the fourteenth century Jews from Germany began to flee south over the Alps—hence the Ashkenazi element still perceptible in Italy today, not in language but in its distinctive religious rite. Around the same time, a comparable migration from southern France reinforced this third great accretion to Italian Jewry. Finally, as already noted, the expulsion of the Jews from Spain and Portugal after 1492 brought the largest contingent ever to arrive on Italy's shores. And the Iberian population was subsequently swelled by coreligionists who had staged through the seaports of the Levant, and by victims of forced conversion, Marranos attracted by the possibility their new homes offered of returning to the faith which in their hearts they had never abandoned.

One could go on to enumerate the successive waves of Jews that were to reach Italy in our own century—from the Balkans, from Nazi Germany, and from the North African Arab world. But these do not belong in this part of our story: the persecutions of 1933-1945 will figure in their proper place later on. Right now it is better to pause and to delineate the salient features of a Jewish tradition so multiform in origin. Its intricate variety emerges most sharply from a glance at a selective roster of Jewish surnames.

In his role as the chronicler of the Jewish community in his native city of Ferrara, an adolescent Giorgio Bassani remarks that Italian Jewish family names all derive from cities and towns, and hence, presumably, are easy to recognize. A friend, significantly enough a Catholic, corrects him: besides the universal "priestly" names of Levi and Cohen, how is one to account for such others as Finzi and Contini—celebrated in another volume by Bassani himself.[3] The objection hits the mark: many names clearly betray their Hebrew origin; many have become so altered over time as to cloud their identity. But the fact remains that place-names account for something like a half: Italian, French, Spanish, Portuguese, Levantine names—and German. These last in their Italianate guise defy detection by the nonspecialist: to cite two families prominent in politics and scholarship, who is to guess that Luzzatti (or Luzzatto) comes from Lausitz, and Morpurgo from Marburg?[4]

Even within Italy itself, place-names as surnames are often those of localities where Jews have not lived for centuries. Indeed, to keep in one's family the name of the city or town from which one had been expelled was a natural way of perpetuating its memory. The history of Italian Jewry has been punctuated by expulsions—in many cases, second moves for those who had fled persecution elsewhere and had reached what they believed to be a secure haven. In the Middle Ages, Sicily and the South had ranked as the major centers of Jewish life, even after they had passed under Aragonese rule. The union of Aragon with Castile ended that: in 1493, the year following Ferdinand and Isabella's decision to rid their own country of Jews, the Jewish population was driven out of Sicily; four decades later, after a tenacious delaying action, in which apparently the Jews enjoyed widespread sympathy among the Catholic majority, they were obliged to depart from the southern mainland also. By the mid-sixteenth century there was scarcely a Jew left south of Rome. And even north of there, in the papal dominions of central Italy, the decrees of successive pontiffs eventually restricted them (with miniscule exceptions) to the three cities of Ancona, Ferrara, and Rome itself.

If such names as Tagliacozzo and Terracini are nostalgically reminiscent of small communities destroyed four hundred years ago, they also bring to mind the resiliency of a population which refused to give up. Such could perhaps be said of Jews everywhere. But what is peculiar to Italy—besides the shift in the Jewish center of gravity from the South to the Center and North—has been the heterogeneity of the cultural memory that all this shuffling about, these arrivals and departures, have entailed. Thus, even for the most secularized of Jews, there has always been *something* precious, some scrap of recollection or family lore which he could latch on to, to sustain him in his moments of despair. The infinite variety of Italian Jewry has offered an unrivaled selection of nostalgic possibilities. It has not been insuperably difficult for those far gone toward assimilation to retrieve a past sufficiently in tune with their longings to convince them that they still were Jews.

Thus, as one community has withered, another has taken its place. In the late sixteenth century, when the protracted process of herding Italy's Jews into ghettos was well under way, there appeared as though by a miracle from on high an oasis of liberty: the free port of Livorno. The Grand Dukes of Tuscany welcomed Jewish merchants, particularly Marranos, to their new emporium: they assured them that they would not live segregated from the rest of the population; that they might trade how and with whom they chose; that they would enjoy virtually full civil rights. And, what is more, the Tuscan rulers kept their promises.

The Italian experience of the ghetto likewise followed no

uniform pattern. If residence in its enclosed, narrow streets was as confining, as crowded, as unhygienic, and as humiliating as elsewhere, both its inception and its duration varied from locality to locality. Broadly speaking, one may say that the institution appeared later and held on longer in Italy than was true in most of Western Europe. To be sure, Jewish quarters had existed since the Middle Ages; but these were simply informal arangements, without official status, and reflecting the preference or convenience of the town authorities and the Jews alike. Their name, *giudecca,* has been preserved on one of Venice's islands. Venice also enjoys the melancholy distinction of having supplied the term for the place of genuine confinement that subsequently spread throughout the Western world: the *ghetto* was the Venetian foundry quarter, where beginning in 1516 the city's Jews were rounded up.

Although Venice took the lead and gave the name to a practice that little by little engulfed the Italian peninsula, it did not provide the chief stimulus for the establishment of ghettos. This came from the Counter-Reformation and from the stern popes who incarnated its persecutory zeal. The key event usually cited is the publication in 1555 of the bull *Cum nimis absurdum* by Paul IV: besides providing for the segregation of the Jews throughout the Papal States, the "infamous bull" and the subsequent decrees that supplemented it codified in minute detail the limitations on their life and work to which the Jewish population was henceforth to be subjected. Under pressure from Rome, the smaller rulers of central and northern Italy followed suit. Florence established its ghetto in 1571, Turin in 1679. By and large, the farther north one went, the more the princes dragged their feet on conforming with papal precedent. But by the end of the seventeenth century there were ghettos nearly everywhere. Only the smaller communities of Piedmont in the far northwest continued to enjoy their freedom for another two or three decades. There was of course the great exception of Livorno—and the contrary exception of the Milanese (like the South, under Spanish rule), where the uncompromising policy of expulsion had prevailed.

A handful of northern communities endured the ghetto experience for little over a century: in Rome this experience dragged on for more than three—the Roman ghetto, which remained intact until 1870, was the last such place of confinement in the Western world to succumb to the forces of emancipation. Overall, as generation after generation lived and labored and died in cramped and dreary quarters, the condition of the Italian Jews deteriorated: they became poorer; their numbers fell; their physique and their morale weakened. By the mid-eighteenth century they had reached their nadir. There was a bitter irony in the fact that just at the point when the spread of Enlightenment elsewhere was beginning to alleviate the Jews' lot, in Italy, which once had ranked as the most welcoming land in all Europe, the old intolerance still held sway.[5]

Nevertheless, it is only fair to add that life in the ghetto, lasting on the average for something like two centuries, figures in retrospect as an episode, if a dreadful one, in a history ten times as long. What is more, here once again the variety of Italian practices came to the aid of the beleaguered Jews. There remained a possibility of movement from ghetto to ghetto, and of these a few were less depressing than the majority. The Venetian regulations, to cite an eminent example, permitted friendly contact between Jews and Christians, whether local inhabitants or foreign visitors. In the gradations of treatment the Jews received, their communities were scattered along a wide continuum, with one pole in Rome, where conditions were at their worst, and the other in Venice, where their situation has been labeled "passable."[6] The smaller ghettos at the very least succeeded in providing better sanitation than the overcrowded quarters of the great cities. And it was these, as we shall subsequently observe in the case of Piedmont, that left behind memories which were not uniformly evil. Such was the final irony of the Italian ghettos: in rare and privileged instances, those dank abodes might shimmer in the sentimentalizing glow of recollection as warm and cozy nooks—and hence as an emotional resource worth preserving long after the threshold of assimilation had been crossed.

I have posed the question of what is left of identity when language and religion are gone. In both these respects the Italian experience differed markedly from the more familiar one of Eastern Europe. A second and a third hypothesis about the tenacity of a residual ethnic consciousness among Italy's Jews derive from reflections on the speech and the religious tone characteristic of this particular branch of Judaism.

The simplest way to put the matter of language is to say that, as opposed to the Jews of Russia and Poland, those of Italy had no language to lose. When spoken Hebrew died out, no language distinct from that of the majority took its place. Nor was there a special literary vehicle, such as until very recently Yiddish could be, which caught the nuances of Jewish expression. There had been of course the Ladino of the Iberian Sephardics, but by the end of the eighteenth century this had largely disappeared, even in its stronghold of Livorno; in any case, it had functioned as a language of commerce rather than of literature. When Italian Jews wrote, they composed their works either in Hebrew or in standard Italian. When they spoke, they did so in the language of their compatriots—that is, in whichever of Italy's local dialects they heard about them. The speech of the ghetto, however, did not sound quite the same as that in the city outside: it was peppered with Hebrew words; it tended toward archaism (a familiar phenomenon within closed-off communities); above all, it had its own distinctive *cantilena*—literally its "song"—its peculiar cadence or lilt or intonation.[7]

Thus, those who found Italian Jewish speech hard to understand did not always realize that what they were hearing differed in little more than pronunciation from the local vernacular. This difficulty did not seem to run the other way: Italian Jews apparently experienced no trouble in conversing with outsiders. By the same token, when they opted for assimilation, it was with no sense of linguistic betrayal. To pass from ghetto speech to normal Italian speech required no particular effort. Nor did it mean to close off a reservoir of memory: after all, memories of the Italian Jewish communities were linked by the tie of language to the larger world beyond them.

The matter of religion was hardly as simple. But even in this respect, the historical experience of Italy's Jews furnished unusual possibilities of openness or pluralism. From medieval times, one of the distinctive features of Italian Judaism had been the choice of "rites" it offered, as each successive layer of arrivals had kept its own particular variety of worship. By the sixteenth century—and down to the twentieth—the major Jewish centers harbored from five to ten different "schools" or synagogues, usually housed in separate rooms if not always in separate buildings, and a number of the smaller centers had as many as two or three. Their names similarly varied from place to place; but usually there would be an old Italian (or "Roman") rite, an Ashkenazi (or "German"), and some form or forms of Sephardic, known not by that name but divided into component parts, "Castilian," "Catalan-Aragonese," or "Levantine," as the case might be. Curiously enough, however the canticles or prayers might differ among them, all used the soft Sephardic pronunciation of the Hebrew language.

Accustomed as he was to this kind of pluralism in ritual, even the strictly observant Italian might not judge too strenuously a certain laxness among his neighbors. "Italian orthodoxy was at no time as rigid as it was north of the Alps."[8] It is to such relative permissiveness that Jewish historians have ascribed he failure of the Reform movement to catch on in Italy in the nineteenth and twentieth centuries: the religious atmosphere was already such as to make Reform Judaism unnecessary. Here, as elsewhere, emancipation brought in its wake a slippage from the faith, sometimes abrupt, at other times protracted. But in Italy the person who lapsed from Judaism, characteristically an intellectual, did not feel the need of the way station of Reform to ease the shock of his great slide. He made a clean break—but without slamming the doors of the temple. "The Italian Jew . . . considered his own religious crisis as a personal phenomenon: too deep to be healed by a mere reform of ritual, and too transitory to place in jeopardy, by retouching it, the stability of the beliefs and practices . . . of his own brothers in the faith. The modern Italian Jew has found it possible to distance himself from religious observance, but he has been firm about leaving intact the faith from which he was departing."[9]

"Distance himself" (*allontanarsi*) may be exactly the right expression. The Jewish intellectual could move away from his fathers' beliefs; he could go for decades without entering a synagogue. But he did not necessarily lose all feeling for the faith he had deserted. And that faith was waiting for him, both "intact" and permissive, should he ever choose to return.

A fourth and final hypothesis about a residual Jewish consciousness, and the one which requires the most nuanced treatment, springs from the relationship between Judaism and the Roman Catholic faith of the Italian majority. Here the key terms are Catholic ambivalence and mutual interpenetration. Both at first glance may look absurd: how is one to discover any attitude toward Jews remotely positive in a Church which provided the materials for popular anti-Semitism, which resorted to forced baptisms and forced attendance at sermons in an effort to win converts, which subjected the Jews to a bizarre assortment of acts of public humiliation?

On closer consideration, however, the Church's stand, more particularly as exemplified in a long sequence of papal pronouncements, appears vacillating and frequently contradictory. No Catholic denied that the Jews languished in the grip of unpardonable theological error; no one questioned the supreme aim of persuading them to embrace Christianity. But within the bounds of this universally recognized ideal, practice oscillated from century to century between leniency and rigor. The popes refrained from urging that Italian Judaism be extirpated by fire and sword; Italy never experienced the frightfulness of mass slaughter on the Iberian or German model. At times of inflamed popular passion—usually provoked by the age-old charge that a Christian child had been the victim of Jewish ritual murder—the Vatican enjoined calm and a close investigation of the facts. Even when with the

Counter-Reformation the Church swung sharply toward repression, for the most part it spared the Jews its maxiumum punishment; burning alive was reserved for Christian heretics or for those who had lapsed from Catholicism. Hence the only Jews to suffer death at the stake, and only a tiny fraction of the thousands who perished in Spain, were a few of the particularly unfortunate among the much-vexed Marranos.

Before the period of rigor set in, popes had frequently maintained cordial relations with individual Jews, and a succession of Jews had served as papal physicians. Such relations were naturally out of the question during the era of the ghetto. By the end of the nineteenth century, however, they were again possible, and it is a matter of more than anecdotal interest that the great fundamentalist Pope of our own century's opening years—St. Pius X, who condemned both Catholic Modernism and Christian Democracy—regarded several Jewish political leaders as his friends. When informed that Ernesto Nathan had been elected mayor of Rome, he was perturbed far less by Nathan's origins than by his freethinking. "If he weren't a Freemason," the Pope reflected, "he would be better than all the others." "But he is a Jew, Holy Father!" "Yes, . . . but he is a man of honor."[10]

If Pius X was a rockbound conservative, he was also warm and humane. The same is usually not said of the one among his successors who of necessity was most deeply involved in the fate of the Jews, Pius XII (Pacelli), the Pope of the holocaust years. Much has been written of Pacelli's failure to speak out against Hitler's atrocities. Less has been said of how he behaved in his homeland. For Italy—for Rome itself—for perhaps the only place to which his power to enforce his will actually extended, his injunction was *salvare la vita:* save lives. And with excellent results: despite the vigilance of the Nazi occupiers, more than 4,000 Jews were saved in Rome alone by Catholics who gave them shelter.[11]

Pius XII's failings and his accomplishments alike may suggest a characteristic Italian combination of realism and humanity. In Italy, even in the worst times, a common humanity linked Christians and Jews: after all, they had lived alongside each other ever since the days when both had survived as stubborn minorities under the rule of imperial Rome. Except when stirred up by fanatical preachers, Italian Catholics tended to take their Jewish neighbors for granted—or to regard them with a curiosity tinged by respect for their moral meticulousness. (We learn of one rabbi of a small community two generations ago who was frequently referred to as the "bishop of the Jews.")[12] In Italy the line of division between Christian and Jew was never as sharp as it was elsewhere. The walls of the ghetto itself were never as hermetic as they were intended to be. Century by century a quiet process of interpenetration went on between the two faiths. They shared an Italianate *dolcezza* in ritual music: sometimes their hymns betrayed family resemblances.[13] Thus, even when a Jew abandoned his religious culture and tacitly accepted the values of the majority, he did not stray so far from his former spiritual home as did the coreligionist who took a similar course elsewhere. In Italy vestiges of the old faith might linger on.

If one is to write of a "silver age," one must have some image of an age of gold hovering behind it. Historians and folk memory agree on the existence of such an age. Only on its dating do opinions differ. What consensus one can detect clusters around the year 1500. It was then that Italy's Jewish population reached its all-time high—possibly 120,000, slightly more than 1 percent of a total of 11,000,000 and 8 percent of world Jewry—a figure which in relative terms has declined ever since. (Three centuries later, after the harrowing experience of expulsions and the ghetto, it was 34,000; in the mid-1970s, after recovery from the Second World War, it was about 35,000. But in 1800 there were only 18,000,000 Italians in all; by 1975 this number had more than tripled—leaving the Jews at just over a twentieth of 1 percent.)[14]

Population statistics, however, can provide little beyond a confirmation in "hard data" of the memory of a golden age. It is more to the point to ask when it was that Italy's Jews felt themselves least reviled, most respected, closest to acceptance by the majority. The period we conventionally call the Renaissance seems to respond best to such questioning. Here once again a cultural legend concurs with Jewish experience—or at least with that of the Jewish elite. The breadth of view, the freedom from prejudice, characteristically ascribed to the men of the Renaissance benefited the Jews as it did so many others of heterodox manners and opinions. And they in turn relaxed, if ever so little, the rigidity of their own customs in order to grasp the hand of friendship extended to them. In this period we hear of Jewish dancing masters and violinists (one of the latter immortalized by Raphael as the model for Apollo on Mount Parnassus). We also read of enthusiasm among Humanists for the study of Hebrew, which now joined Latin and Greek as a third language required of men of learning. Universities added chairs in Hebrew to their faculties; princely courts engaged the services of scribes and librarians competent in the sacred language of the Jews. By the mid-sixteenth century the promise of cultural symbiosis was luring Christian and Jew alike.[15]

The twin blights of Counter-Reformation and ghetto put a stop to that. And even earlier, the expulsion of the Jews from Sicily and southern Italy had given a foretaste of what was to come. It is with this series of events that disagreements over dating begin: some may argue for placing the golden age before 1493, before the uprooting of so many ancient Jewish settlements; others may advance the claim that the expulsion itself, reinforced by a steady influx from the Iberian peninsula and the Levant, strengthened the Jewish communities of Rome and points north by adding to their membership fresh contingents of exceptional intellectual eminence. On balance, the case for situating the best years just before the mid-sixteenth century sounds the more persuasive. By this time, though the southern half of Italy had been stripped of its Jews, the northern and central half had been enriched by the arrival of the refugees. And the Center and North were precisely the regions equipped to give the new arrivals the welcome to Renaissance culture they longed for; the cities to which the south Italian and the Spanish Jews fled—Rome, Ferrara, and the rest—ranked as the major focuses of art and learning, and in these activities non-Christians were at long last free to participate.

However it may be delimited, the age of gold, if such it was, figures as tragically brief. Yet the experience of the late fifteenth and early sixteenth centuries left behind it indelible traces in the Italian Jewish consciousness. It bequeathed to succeeding generations the notion of and the aspiration toward mutual adaptation with their non-Jewish neighbors—the notion, almost unique in the diaspora, of an "open" Jewish community, "imbued" with the culture of the milieu surounding it, and the aspiration toward a synthesis between-traditional Judaism and the values of Italian Humanism.

Efforts in this direction, although constantly disappointed, never ceased entirely. Their end result was a mentality that has been described as "ecumenical-humanist-progressive," a mentality, moreover, distrustful of all forms of clericalism, even in Jewish guise.[16] Here once more we find the now familiar syndrome of the Jew impatient to cast off the armor of traditional observances, thirsting to enter into friendly relations with the Christians and the freethinkers he saw about him, yet at the same time reluctant—indeed, refusing—to grant that he was no longer a Jew.

Was this aspiration achieved in what one may call a second golden age, the age of full emancipation? The question defies a simple answer. Yet one may at the very least outline its contours by breaking it down into its three main components: the nature of the emancipation; the extent of a lingering anti-Semitism; and the emotional resonance for the Jews themselves of the perils and the attractions of assimilation.

The emancipation of Italy's Jews came about piecemeal over a period of nearly ninety years. Paradoxically enough, the process started in what had once ranked as the most benighted region of the North: the Milanese or Lombardy. Here Spanish rule had brought about, although a half-century later than in the South, the expulsion of all but an insignificant remnant of Jewish families. In 1714, with the transfer of Milan to Austria, it again became possible for Jews to live in Lombardy, and a small number began to trickle back. And these in turn received the delightful surprise of a sudden and unexpected gift from above: the Toleration Patent issued in 1781 by the reforming Emperor Joseph II.

There followed in the late 1790s the "false dawn" of emancipation under the auspices of the French. For two decades after Bonaparte's tumultuous descent into the north Italian plain the peninsula's Jews, with sporadic interruptions, were to enjoy the blessings of civil equality. Most of them profited from their new freedom to the full, and occasionally with an exuberance which disconcerted their Christian neighbors. By and large, however, Italy's urban bourgeoisie welcomed the liberal provisions symbolized by the battering down of the ghetto's gates. And by the same token, people who could now at last enter without reservation into friendly relations with Jews accustomed themselves so rapidly to the change that they were far from happy to see it revoked. With the fall of Napoleon and the restoration of the former sovereigns in 1815, the old limitations on Jewish rights were also in theory restored. But their application varied in rigor from state to state and from city to city: local authorities winked at violations or devised loopholes for escape from the letter of the law. In Rome alone, not unexpectedly, the papal government remained intransigent.[17]

From 1848 on, the mounting recognition of the absurdity, impracticality, and inhumanity of the old restrictions began to sweep them away in a torrent that soon turned to a flood. By 1860, with Italy's unification, the last vestiges disappeared—except in beleaguered Rome, where the Jews had to wait another decade. And the same torrential character marked the Jewish acceptance of emancipation: the ghetto's inhabitants burst forth into the wide world outside; the more talented and ambitious threw themselves with enthusiasm into the activities and professions from which they had previously been barred. In countless cases a single generation sufficed to bring individual Jews to the forefront of whatever calling they had chosen. Emancipation had been so long delayed, had been marred by so many false starts and disappointments, that its final achievement was greeted by Jew and non-Jew alike as simply the normal and civilized thing to do. Perhaps to no other European people did it come with so little resistance from the majority and so much gratitude from its beneficiaries.

Before the turn of the century Italy's Jews appeared fully integrated into the national life. Still more, their leading personalities constituted a special and respected variety of elite. Jews were distinguishing themselves in science, in scholarship—and in politics. The first Jew to achieve eminence in public affairs was Isacco Artom, private secretary to the architect of unification, Count Camillo di Cavour; Artom's descendants were to rank high among the small roster of Italy's ennobled Jewish families. By the early twentieth century one half-Jew and one full Jew were figuring among the prime ministers whose brief incumbency now and then interrupted the long rule of Giovanni Giolitti. Sidney Sonnino was a Protestant, Luigi Luzzatti a freethinker. But if Sonnino can scarcely be counted among Italy's Jewish notables, Luzzatti explicitly and forthrightly acknowledged his antecedents. In 1909, in reply to a query by a Socialist parliamentary leader, he characterized himself as an "unrepetant deist." "But through a faith in freedom of conscience," which was at the center of his being and which invariably put him "on the side of those oppressed and despised for religious reasons," he returned "to being a Jew every time" someone acused him of "being one."[18] It would be hard to find a pithier expression of what I have earlier called a "residual Jewish consciousness."

From these prime ministries of the years 1906-1911 one may date the generation, ending in the mid-1920s, of Italian Jewry's second golden age, the two decades in which Jews loomed largest in the national life. By the end of that period their numbers had risen to more than 40,000. Two dozen were sitting among their country's elder statesmen in the royally nominated Senate. Eight percent of the university professors were Jewish; 6.7 percent of those whose names figured in the standard handbook of contemporary biography were of similar origin—and this from a pool of Jews constituting only a tenth of 1 percent of the total population.[19]

Did such success mean that anti-Semitism had vanished from Italian soil? Once again a nuanced answer is in order. At the very least one can say that whatever hostility to the Jews remained was almost entirely religiously based; the "racial" anti-Semitism which had begun to appear in late-nineteenth-century Germany had no Italian counterpart. Polemics directed against Italian Judaism, usually the work of obscure, half-educated priests, flared up and sputtered out periodically; most of them did not rise above the level of the vulgar, cruel jokes with which schoolboys sometimes mocked their Jewish fellow-pupils. A more sustained line of reasoning enlivened the columns of the Jesuit organ *Civiltà Cattolica*. For its clerical editors, Freemasonry loomed as the menace linking Judaism with unbelief. In this case the charge was not without some slim basis in fact: at the turn of the century the Italian Masons'supreme council included among its forty-one members seven Jews—the chief of whom was the Grand Master himself, Ernesto Nathan, the future mayor of Rome and friend of Pius X.[20]

But this sort of association with non-Jewish freethinkers and anticlericals was uncharacteristic of Italy's leading Jews. The dominant attitude had emerged a quarter-century earlier from a curious sequence of events which in retrospect figures as the nearest that pre-Fascist Italy ever came to a Dreyfus

Case, and its mildness testifies to the lower level of hostility to Jews among the Italians as compared with the French. In mid-1873, just after the incoming prime minister, Marco Minghetti, had submitted for royal approval the name of a prominent and respected Venetian Jew, Senator Isacco Pesaro Maurogonato, as minister of finance, another Venetian, the obscure deputy Francesco Pasqualigo, telegraphed to King Victor Emmanuel II his strong objections to the appointment. Everything about the case looked odd—more particularly, the boldness of a direct appeal to the sovereign, plus the fact that Pasqualigo's record marked him as a left-liberal rather than a clerical. He himself maintained that "religious intolerance" had nothing to do with his stand; his opposition to Maurogonato sprang from "exclusively political" motives—that is to say, his conviction that Jews were bound by a "double nationality" and hence were unqualified to serve as ministers. For his part, the Venetian senator declined the appointment, alleging family concerns. Only at the very end of the year, and after mounting agitation in his behalf, did he inform the King of his real reason, that it would be "inopportune" for a non-Catholic to take responsibility for applying the stringent financial measures of the new Italian state with regard to religious bodies.

Had Maurogonato's decision gone the other way, the King was prepared, even eager, to support him; so, apparently, was the prime minister and most of Italy's governing elite. (Again the parallel with Captain Dreyfus is instructive.) The argument Pasqualigo had advanced was not unfamiliar to Italian liberals: some shared his qualms about "double nationality" in a newly unified country which was still resting on shaky foundations. But what they really feared was the potential disloyalty of the clericals; in the liberals' minds, the Jews' divided allegiance, if such it was, ranked as incomparably less preoccupying. And the leaders of Italian Jewry proved more than willing to reassure them on this score with effusive professions of patriotic devotion.

The dénouement is the truly significant aspect of the Maurogonato-Pasqualigo affair. What started as an isolated manifestation of "political" anti-Semitism ended with a gesture designed to ward off the danger that an eminent Jew might stand accused of hostility to the Church.[21] In his reluctance to arouse the sleeping dogs of religious anti-Semitism, Maurogonato was typical of Italian Jews who had entered public life and who repeatedly refrained from adding to the bitterness that already marked Church-state relations. On the contrary, they went out of their way to adopt a conciliatory tone toward Catholicism as a faith and as an institution. Thus, although Jews could be found across the whole political spectrum, they tended to cluster around moderate liberal-conservatism; they inclined less often to the Left than was true elsewhere. Not until the twentieth century were they to play a prominent role in Italian Socialism—and as moderate Socialists in the person of Claudio Treves and Giuseppe Emanuele Modigliani (the older brother of Amedeo the painter).

By that time the dominant political attitude among Italian Jewry had begun to bring rewards. The "open" and even friendly stance of the new pope, Pius X (1903-1914), had helped. So too had a readiness on the part of the Jewish political elite to cooperate with clericals in combatting atheism and in opposing their country's one effort prior to 1970 to legalize divorce. This bizarre rapprochement culminated in 1913 with the support the clericals gave two Jewish candidates for the Chamber of Deputies, candidates bearing the illustrious names of Morpurgo and Artom.[22] By the outbreak of the First

World War, Catholic, religiously based anti-Semitism—at least on the higher levels of society—appeared all but dead.

If "racial" reasons for hostility to the Jews were absent, and religious reasons seemed on the point of disappearing, were there any other grounds left? It has been argued that the familiar resentment of Jewish economic power, which figured so prominently in Germany, was far from negligible in Italy. Certainly Jewish firms held leading positions in banking, in insurance, and in publishing—but scarcely on a German scale. They did dominate a few localities, the most familiar example being the position of the Olivetti typewriter family in the small Piedmontese town of Ivrea. Yet such evidence remains fragmentary and unconvincing. It is more relevant to suggest that the urban economic "presence" of the Jews was "perceptible" in only one major city, Trieste, which prospered, although "unredeemed" from Austrian rule, beyond Italy's borders until 1919, and in a few smaller (and historic) centers of Jewry such as Venice, Livorno, Ancona, and Ferrara.[23] And even in these, the Jews kept a low profile: most of the time they made themselves as inconspicuous as possible; by and large they were known for their quiet, dignified manners and bearing.

All of which is to say that by 1914 the process of assimilation had gone very far indeed. Eight years later, when Mussolini came to power, it had gone farther still: in contrast to so many Italians who had harbored neutralist or even defeatist sentiments about their country's intervention in the First World War, the Jewish middle class, not unpredictably, had ranked as superpatriotic. How deep did this assimilation go? What was its emotional resonance? These are the final and most baffling questions we are left with in assessing the residual strength of Jewish identity on threshold of Facism.

It is here that Italian historians and memoirists diverge radically one from another. For the most vigorous and challenging of contemporary memoirists, the "great slide from emancipation toward assimilation" looms in retrospect as a colossal mistake: the Jews' low profile betrayed their sense of "guilt at having been closed up in ghettos for so many centuries" and their "constant preoccupation" lest their "gratitude" for their liberation therefrom "might never have been adequately expressed." For the most exhaustive chronicler of the individual achievements of the Jewish elite, such deeds and writings deserve to be celebrated with a joyous, if restrained pride, as an "honor to Italian civilization." The reader may take his choice—while noting that even the stern critic is obliged to recognize that the "Jewish intellectual bourgeoisie," although "plunged up to the neck in . . . assimilation, . . . still remained tied in some fashion or other, on occasion, without knowing how or why, to the ancestral 'religion.' "[24]

The advocates and the opponents of assimilation were to clash at a meeting of Jewish youth held in Livorno in November 1924. The date in itself is significant: five months earlier the outspokenly anti-Fascist deputy Giacomo Matteotti had been found murdered; two months later Mussolini assumed "full responsibility" for what had occurred and began to recast his two-year-old rule in a fully authoritarian style. The year 1924 marked an ideological and cultural watershed; with its fateful concluding months our story begins.

The young men who argued with each other so fervently in Livorno could not possibly know what the future held in store for them. For the time being they seemed in passionate disagreement: the fledgling historian Nello Rosselli, offspring of a leading Florentine family, spoke for intellectuals who had rejected the traditional observances; Enzo Sereni, whose Roman antecedents were almost equally distinguished, told what it meant for himself and a handful of others to find their way back to the spiritual world of their ancestors by the Zionist path. Already, however, the two agreed more than they knew: both were determined, if quiet, anti-Fascists; both, like Matteotti, were eventually to be slaughtered for their beliefs. Still more, both were reluctant to push their differences of opinion to an irreconcilable confrontation: Sereni would never deny that he was an Italian any more than Rosselli would disavow his Jewish heritage.[25]

Is this merely to say that each in his own way wanted to have his cake and eat it too? Not quite; that would be far too simple. In Italy the young men and women who embraced Zionism continued to be steeped in their country's culture. Like the greatest of their mentors, Dante Lattes, they spoke and wrote Italian with love and elegance; for them Hebrew remained a second language, frequently acquired with pain and seldom fully mastered. (In the supreme crisis of German occupation in the Second World War, Enzo Sereni was to return from his adopted homeland in Palestine to share the fate of his own people.) For their part, the more sensitive of the assimilated refused to scorn or to mock the little world they had left behind. However securely ensconced they might feel in the wide world of Italian society, they did not try to forget that they were Jews—Jews by the light of their own ultrapermissive interpretation, but Jews nonetheless. Doubly shielded by their twin identities, they embraced both.

The year 1924 has a further meaning. In an Italy which shone as a great success story of Jewish emancipation, where on balance the Jewish experience had been one of the happiest in the entire diaspora, where in half the country ordinary people "had no idea what the Jews were, since there weren't any" to be seen, where in the other half to be Jewish was regarded as an "interesting curiosity," an "amiable eccentricity rather than a social mistake," where Jews were simply those who went to synagogue rather than to church, indistinguishable from their neighbors in physical appearance, behavior, and speech—to such an extent that foreign Jews sometimes doubted whether they should be reckoned Jews at all—in the Italy of the early twentieth century there was still one field in which Jews had failed to distinguish themselves.[26] Curiously enough, although Italian Jewry had produced generals and even naval officers—something unheard-of elsewhere—it had not yet bred an imaginative writer of international renown. Sabatino Lopez had won popularity as a playwright; Enrico Castelnuovo, in his novel *I Moncalvo* (1908), had depicted with scrupulous objectivity the milieu of upper bourgeois Jewish families. But by and large the Italian Jews who had tried their hand at literature had ranked as no more than "Sunday writers," talented amateurs without a deeply felt vocation.[27]

Then quite unexpectedly at the beginning of 1924 James Joyce began a campaign on behalf of his close friend Italo Svevo's *The Confessions of Zeno* that was to bring its author a glorious *succès d'estime;* not since Alessandro Manzoni's *I promessi sposi,* of a century earlier, had an Italian novel been so warmly praised abroad. Svevo, already past sixty and disabused by the fate of two previous books which had fallen flat, scarcely knew what to make of his sudden fame. He was also far from sure that he liked being a Jew. Yet the eminence which had overwhelmed him marked another kind of watershed: from this point on, writers of Jewish origin were for a half-century to bulk disproportionately large on the Italian literary scene.

How did the change come about? Slowly, tentatively these authors learned to understand themselves and, along with themselves, their heritage as Jews. They "acquired a sincerity, a pride, a courage that . . . the . . . epigoni of the ghetto did not possess," a "frankness" and a "habit of plain speaking and introspection, in a word," a "new dignity."[28] In their biographies they faithfully mirrored the social and cultural peculiarities of the milieu from which they derived. With one exception they had grown up in big cities; their forebears had usually come from the smaller communities that had begun to shrivel as the pull of the major centers for the newly emancipated had become irresistible. But such displacements had left relatives behind or family members who had moved to different cities—hence far-flung kinship networks sedulously maintained and cultivated. Several of the writers in question were the product of marriages with non-Jews or were to contract similar unions themselves, or both together, and this in a country where by the late 1930s nearly half the marriages of Jews were mixed and where to marry a Jew was frequently esteemed a sign of upward mobility.[29] In these circumstances religious practice tended to lapse. Yet sometimes not entirely: the extent of observance among Jewish literary figures ran the gamut from none at all to a tender respect for tradition not too far removed from orthodoxy.

In what follows I propose to discuss six prose writers in their varying urban settings. Besides the great forerunner Svevo, I shall be dealing with the early work of Alberto Moravia and with the reminiscences and the novels of Carlo Levi, Primo Levi, Natalia Ginzburg, and Giorgio Bassani.

Their lives span four cities—Trieste, Rome, Turin, and Ferrara—differing markedly one from another in their history as communities of Jews and in their contemporary tone. The vicissitudes undergone by these men and this woman intersect only now and then—notably in the period after Mussolini lunged into anti-Semitism. Yet certain early experiences they do have in common: they are all from the middle classes—nearly always from the *professional* middle class—all assimilated, all with a rich cultural endowment.

Something, some submerged thread, must bind them together. It is this hidden (or private) connection I am seeking. Needless to say, it is nothing conceptually so primitive as a Jewish (or even an Italian Jewish) ethnic "character." It is rather a matter of shared sensibility—what Ludwig Wittgenstein would call a "family resemblance," adding that its boundaries need not be precisely defined or circumscribed.[30] On the continuum of such a sensibility Moravia stands at one end, Bassani at the other. Between these poles lies the vast and troubled expanse in which a residual Jewish consciousness managed to survive, constantly sinking, constantly resurfacing and sinking again, but never without leaving a trace behind.

2

Exercises in Futility: Trieste and Rome

Why "futility"? The first prose writers of Jewish origin to win critical acclaim—Italo Svevo and Alberto Moravia—were far from convinced that their Jewishness had anything positive about it. Both baptized Catholics, they rarely spoke of their antecedents, and for the most part only when asked about them. This shared reluctance sprang from rather different sources—in Svevo's case from emotional discomfort, in Moravia's from an absence of Jewish memories or associations. To both of them it seemed futile to call oneself a Jew—just as in their novels the theme of the futility of life in general was to return again and again. Was there a link between these two meanings of the word? Did Svevo's and Moravia's sense of the irrelevance of being Jewish reinforce their personal pessimism, their disenchantment with a world devoid of ultimate meaning? This question must be held in abeyance until we come to younger writers in whose work a note of hope was to ring out loud and clear through the infernal din of unimaginable calamity.

Possibly figures so uncertain about their Jewishness do not belong in our story at all. But to pass them over would not only be to deny to the Jewish tradition any part in the formation or sensibility of Italy's two most celebrated twentieth-century novelists; it would be to omit an indispensable prologue to a consideration of subsequent writers on whom the Jewish experience—even when painful, or perhaps particularly when painful—acted as a spur to creativity. Svevo and Moravia loom too large to be brushed aside. So too do the cities whose streets and parks and piazzas gave their work its characteristic, its unmistakable pith and tang.

The "Redeemed" and the Eternal City

In 1924, when Svevo's fame began, his native city of Trieste had been "redeemed" from the Austrians for only a half-decade. Ironically enough, this consummation of patriotic longings, which had helped to stimulate Svevo's own flagging literary energies, was to prove the city's commercial and cultural downfall. By the time *The Confessions of Zeno* appeared, the *ambiente* it explored was already fast disappearing.

As the Austro-Hungarian empire's only great seaport, Trieste before 1914 had constituted a unique social phenomenon. Trilingual, it was cosmopolitan by tradition and necessity: German was the language of administration; Italian that of trade and of the city's majority; Slovene the speech of the peasants in its hinterland. It lived and breathed a passion for business. Yet the city's apparent absorption with ships and stocks and balance sheets did not exclude a respect for literature and the arts: Svevo was subsequently to characterize it as "singularly adapted to all forms of spiritual cultivation."[1] One essential prop to it cultural life, however, it notably lacked: a university of it own. Hence when it came time for his higher education, the intellectually aspiring Triestino faced a difficult choice: he might cross the nearby frontier and study in Italy, with Florence the most frequent goal; or he might remain within the Hapsburg dominions and go to Vienna or some other German-speaking center. Most of the literati did the former (and came back with their Italian suitably polished, their hearts vibrant with irredentism); scientists, engineers, and physicians tended to take the latter course (thereby condemning themselves forever to speaking dialect rather than standard Italian). Svevo did neither. He had gone to work at the age of nineteen. But his mentality remained closer to that of the Vienna-oriented than to that of his literary peers: fluent in German, he never learned to write Italian to the satisfaction of the linguistic purists, and his irredentism was intermittent and tinged with skepticism.

That Svevo should have taken English lessons from the expatriate Irishman James Joyce ranks as a heaven-sent accident. That he should have dabbled in the writings of Sigmund Freud was virtually foreordained. Both his Germanic cultural orientation and his Jewish origin inclined him in that direction. For him, as for a nucleus of fellow-Triestini, these mutually reinforcing influences combined to make their city an outpost of Vienna. Svevo knew and respected the first genuine Italian psychoanalyst, Edoardo Weiss, who had studied in the Austrian capital with the master himself. And, as elsewhere in the early days of psychoanalysis, the handful of others who took Weiss's profession seriously for the most part came from Jewish backgrounds.[2]

To be a Jew in Trieste meant something perceptibly different from what it did in Italy proper. For one thing, the Adriatic seaport's Jewish population remained as mixed as Italy's once had been: besides the bilingual, German-educated element, there was a steady influx of new arrivals from the eastern Mediterranean. For another, this population was more numerous: 4 percent of the total—high by Italian standards, low by Austrian. Finally, emancipation had come earlier here than to any other major Italian-speaking Jewish community—as a result of the Emperor Joseph II's Toleration Patent, from which the tiny Milanese community had also profited. In 1784 the locks on the gates of Trieste's ghetto had been removed, and by the nineteenth century Jews were playing a leading role in the city's commercial, intellectual, and administrative life.

Meantime the old ghetto had continued to exist—not in the sense of a place of confinement, but rather as the quarter in which traditionally minded Jews still preferred to live. The best introduction to this enclave of an earlier age may be found in the reminiscences of Svevo's younger literary colleague, the poet Umberto Poli (who changed his surname to the more Hebrew-sounding Saba, while simultaneously figuring as one of Weiss's patients). A corresponding mixture of respect for the past and modern-mindedness marked his memories of his native city. For Saba, to recall the old ghetto he had known as a child—or better, whose lore he had inbibed from his beloved aunt—meant to inject a "note of color" into his surroundings, to depict the exotic diversity of a way of life which had vanished. It was in a half-mocking tone, with accents of the grotesque, that he told of a "marvelous world," richly furnished with stage props like the red fez his uncle wore. This tone, as Saba realized after the Second World War, when he finally published what he had written four decades earlier, was suited to the more innocent era immediately prior to 1914; then anti-Semitism had seemed a mere "jest," and one could still "without remorse" indulge in an "understanding irony, veined with hidden tenderness."[3] In a subsequent generation—of an age to be Saba's children—such memories would prompt a more affirmative tone of lyricism and nostalgia.

By that time Trieste had long ago lost both its Jewish "color" and its economic and cultural eminence. In joining Italy, it had forefeited the commercial hinterland that had enriched it and the cosmopolitan spirit that had given it a distinctive flavor. The patriotism of the Triestini had been their undoing. Yet the paradoxical combination of a waning of indigenous cultural vigor and the closer, more sustained contact with the major centers of Italian thought and writing which had now become possible produced the *Zeno* phenomenon. The reluctantly Jewish, half-Germanized Svevo could figure at last as the *Italian* novelist he had always longed to be.

In bestowing their allegiance on Italy, Trieste's Jews had also assumed their rightful place as numerically third among the country's Jewish communities. The first of course was Rome. If the capital both of the nation and of Catholicism called itself eternal, its Jewish inhabitants could make a similar boast: they felt they had lived in Rome forever.

Trieste's was the first ghetto burst open by the torrent of emancipation; Rome's was the last. Nowhere in Italy were the rewards of emancipation grasped so eagerly, so tumultuously, as in the somnolent papal city which the arrival of the national government after 1870 had suddenly stirred to life. The period immediately previous, however, ranked among the worst that the Roman Jews had endured. By the 1860s they had sunk into the torpor of despair: overcrowding and periodic flooding from the Tiber had defeated their efforts at sanitation; they had barely checked the cholera that had raged through the ghetto at the end of the decade.[4] By the 1880s this same ghetto had become unrecognizable: its crumbling, unhygienic dwellings were being systematically demolished; Rome's age-old Jewish quarter had succumbed to the plan of modernization by which the municipal council was attempting to keep pace with the voracious demand for housing and office space that the city's promotion to the status of national capital had entailed.

The Roman Jews' reaction to their uprooting varied radically, and perhaps predictably, along class lines. The poorer and less-educated apparently resented the condemnation of buildings to which, however constricted and rickety, they had been accustomed for countless generations. After a few years of living in unfamiliar quarters, they began to move back to their former dwelling place, now protected from floods by a recently constructed embankment. Thus, what Romans of all descriptions continued to call the ghetto reestablished itself in its newly tidied and straightened streets and those immediately adjacent.[5] And when it came time to build a modern synagogue to replace a jumble of five old ones that had been destroyed by fire, it seemed only natural to locate it facing the Tiber in the quarter where the Jews had always lived. The scale and massiveness of the new temple, dedicated in 1904, attested to the wealth the community had acquired in a single generation. Viewed from one of Rome's commanding heights, its square cupola bulked larger than any other feature of the city's skyline except for the neighboring and equally modern Victor Emmanuel monument and the dome of St. Peter's itself.[6]

At Sabbath services the great synagogue was crowded with the little folk, the *popolani,* of the quarter it dominated. In the early 1930s a new arrival from the north found himself disoriented by the noise and bustle, the plebeian character of the throng in and around the temple. In his own home community the congregation had been quieter and more middle class —and smaller, so small that it had sometimes proved difficult to muster the ritually prescribed quota of ten adult males! In Rome he felt as though he were "in a cathedral."[7] For after the turn of the century Rome was unique among Italian cities in having retained a Jewish quarter in the old sense—and with it nearly one-third the country's Jewish population.

Ten years after the completion of the main synagogue, another was opened beyond the Forum on the Viminal Hill. The location in itself tells a great deal about the sociology of the emancipated Roman Jews. The richer and the more educated—and frequently less observant—preferred to move to higher ground outside the ghetto quarter. The families whose sons were now entering the mainstream of Italian life in an explosive charge of pent-up talent wanted to give visible form to their newly acquired status as equal citizens by living intermingled with the non-Jewish majority. But a number of them, at least initially, did not want to move too far. A characteristic compromise was that of Angelo Sereni, who in the 1890s became president of the Jewish community and almost simultaneously built for his widely extended family a splendid five-story residence on the Via Cavour, a street which offered the twin advantages of modernity and easy walking distance from the former ghetto.[8]

Besides old Roman families such as the Sereni, a host of recent arrivals had settled in the newer quarters of the city. Once Rome had become the national capital it exercised a magnetic effect on aspiring Jews from all over the country; within two generations its Jewish population more than doubled. Elsewhere, notably in Piedmont, as the old restrictions lapsed, a regional center sucked the lifeblood of the smaller communities surrounding it; yet the Jews who had moved to the big city still lived close enough to maintain some contact with their original home towns. In Rome it was otherwise: the small communities nearby had been dispersed three centuries earlier. Hence the Jews who arrived in the capital came from a distance and left their old associations far behind. Many of them never, or only fleetingly, enrolled as full-fledged members of Rome's Jewish community; they never became *Roman* Jews in the same sense as those whose ancestors had lived on the banks of the Tiber from time immemorial.[9] In sum, a triple cleavage—of social class, of religious observance, and of date of arrival—split the city's Jewish population into sharply contrasting mentalities.

Among the more recent arrivals was the father of Alberto Pincherle, who at an early age chose to write under the pen name of Moravia. The Pincherle family ranked with the leading Jews of Venice; assimilated for the better part of a century, it had distinguished itself in scholarship and public service. The novelist's father, in contrast, was an architect and engineer, who helped "develop" still a third quarter of Jewish settlement in Rome: the area of villas and small apartment houses near the parkland of the Villa Borghese, which at the turn of the century was still suburban in atmosphere.

This was the quarter of Moravia's native city (he himself was Roman-born) that he naturally knew best; in novel after novel he was to delineate with mordant precision its worldliness, its self-indulgence, its futility. As he grew older, however—and particularly after the crucial experience of being sheltered by poor people during the Second World War—he widened his range to include all classes of his city's population. In the series of sketches entitled *Roman Tales* which he published in the 1950s he ranged from hills to flatland, from bank to bank of the Tiber, with each shop or tavern or dwelling given its exact location. Like Svevo, he loved the physical detail of his city; he invariably offered his reader a concrete image of where the action was going on. But no more than in the case of Svevo, did Jews as such figure in his account; although Moravia's imagination eventually felt at home in Rome's plebeian quarters, it never seemed to come to rest in the old ghetto. That particular assignment—to write with a corresponding topographical meticulousness of the life of Jews themselves—was to await Giorgio Bassani's bittersweet celebration of his native Ferrara.

Italo Svevo's "Discomfort": Premature Aging and Belated Fame

James Joyce, long ago departed from Trieste but still occasionally corresponding with his old friend Svevo, proved an effective propagandist. While in Italy itself *The Confessions of Zeno* was winning scarcely more acclaim than its two predecessors, the tenacious Irishman was pushing and prodding his French literary confreres into recognition of a masterpiece. The novel had been published (at the author's expense) in late 1923. By the following January, Joyce had launched his promotional campaign. Exactly a year later, Svevo received the first of a series of admiring letters from Paris. And it was by a ricochet effect from the French that Italian critics finally awoke to the importance of what their newly acquired countryman had produced. The one destined for the greatest eminence, the young poet Eugenio Montale, knew nothing of Svevo until on a visit to Paris in 1925 he heard the name repeatedly mentioned with respect. Returning home, he devoured all three novels and sat down to write the first "authoritative" discussion of the Triestino's work to appear in any country.[10]

At least one Italian, then, had a right to debate the primacy of the French in the "discovery" of Svevo. For their part, the Parisian literati found a ready-made tag to pin on the author of *Zeno:* he was the Italian counterpart of their own recently deceased Marcel Proust. When the English-speaking world in turn discovered Svevo, he became the Italian Joyce—as for readers of German he was to become later still the Italian Musil. All this is familiar literary history, the history of the interior monologue in early-twentieth-century fiction. Svevo himself welcomed such flattering comparisons: after a lifetime of neglect, and likening himself to a "baby 64 years old," he basked with naive enjoyment in his unfamiliar good fortune. His pleasure turned out to be pathetically brief: after less than a half-decade of fame, he was killed by an auto accident in the late summer of 1928.

Thus it was only natural that for most of his readers he remained a man of mystery. Ever since his death, his critics have been tormenting themselves with a pair of riddles. For all his international renown, was he truly a master of the Italian language? How Jewish was he, if he seldom mentioned his origins and wrote novels devoid of Jewish characters? The questions are linked, since both speak to the matter of personal and literary identity. The second alone, however, directly concerns us now. And this in turn may best be explored by looking first at Svevo's biography and then at the novels themselves.

Svevo's references to his Jewishness are summed up (and perhaps exhausted) by two lapidary utterances: a comment on

Franz Kafka that to be a Jew was not a "comfortable position," and the more cryptic "It isn't race which makes a Jew, it's life!"[11] His own life had clearly begun as that of a Jew; his brief description of his father as "assimilated" gave a good deal less than half the story.[12] In fact, both father and mother were observant, in their own relaxed fashion, and the former attained to an exalted position in his temple. Such details, however, we would never learn from reading Svevo; they may be found in references scattered through the diary of his younger brother Elio—for example, to the school run by a rabbi which the boys attended and to a network of relatives with Italian-Jewish names.[13] Almost the only "foreign" surname is the one Svevo originally bore, Schmitz, and herewith the complexities in his heritage begin.[14]

His father's family derived from Germany, his mother's from Trieste. It appears that this father, a self-made businessman, moved a further step up in the social scale by marrying into the well-established Moravia clan. But he never allowed his offspring to forget their German-speaking lineage, and he insisted that his sons learn the language correctly. Hence the future Svevo—called throughout his life by family and friends by his real name of Ettore Schmitz—was shipped off at the age of eleven to a boarding school near Würzburg. Its clientele consisted mostly of the sons of German-Jewish businessmen: in this company the boy Ettore spent five years, amply sufficient to perfect his German and to steep himself in its classics.

Against such a background it may seem curious that it had become his profoundest desire to cut a figure in Italian literature, a desire frustrated for more than four decades. In 1880, two years after his return from boarding school, his father suffered a financial collapse—so much for Ettore's dream of bringing his literary Italian up to the level of his German by a protracted stay in Italy. Instead, he was condemned to drudgery, for the most part as a bank clerk. Doggedly pursuing his literary ambitions, improving his written Italian as best he could, he drew on his own bitter experience in his first novel, *A Life,* published in 1892.

Meantime, what of his Jewishness? It had gone underground. He had ceased to be either observant or believing and had settled into a lifetime hostility to all forms of organized religion. Yet when it came to the acid test of marriage, he turned to a Jewish family. Like his father, he married "up"—and into a branch of the very same family. In 1896 he won as his bride his first cousin once removed, Livia Veneziani, whose mother's maiden name had been Moravia. Two years later his second novel, *Senilità (As a Man Grows Older),* appeared. In this case once more, as with its predecessor, the Italian literary public failed to take notice. The man who wrote under the pseudonym of Svevo drew the logical and melancholy conclusion: he put aside his literary aspirations and little by little became a successful, if eccentric and unorthodox, businessman in the service of his father-in-law, Gioachino Veneziani.

Svevo's marriage lifted him into comfortable financial circumstances. His father-in-law, as a young man working for *his* father-in-law, had invented the "Moravia anti-fouling composition," a paint devised to protect the keels of ships from barnacles and corrosion, manufactured by a secret process, which brought prosperity to the family enterprises. (Umberto Saba has narrated with restrained hilarity the informal way in which Svevo, uncertain of his English and not yet coached by Joyce, succeeded in negotiating, after only five minutes of conversation, a major contract with the British Admiralty.)[15]

Marriage also confused whatever sense of Jewishness still remained with him. The inventor's father-in-law—Svevo's uncle—had made the "mistake" of marrying an Austrian Catholic. Their daughter, Svevo's future mother-in-law, had been brought up in the Catholic faith, as was her own daughter Livia. The one "taint" of Christianity in an otherwise Jewish family proved indelible. During her first year of marriage Livia suffered grievously from what she believed to be her "sin" in having wedded a Jew. The birth of a daughter put matters right for her. Seriously ill after her delivery, she inspired in her impetuous, warm-hearted, *and* passive husband a wish to make amends: he went off to a priest for baptism.

A quarter-century later the golden-haired Livia was to serve as a model for Joyce's Anna Livia Plurabelle. Some critics have also detected traces of her husband in the Leopold Bloom of *Ulysses.* What is undeniable is that Svevo helped Joyce with the specific details his friend needed for composing a Jewish character.[16] So at the very least one can say that he did not try to forget or to deny his heritage. But if Svevo continued to think of himself as a Jew—something his wry and pithy references to the fact would confirm—it was as a Jew of an idiosyncratic variety. Though he aspired to be an Italian writer, he conformed to no recognizable Italian Jewish pattern. His upbringing and his education had been too German for that. He himself sealed this double identity in the choice of a pen name which translates as "Italus the Swabian." He did not add the third identity that underlay them both.

❧

It is of more than anecdotal interest that Svevo's first published piece of writing was a newspaper article on Shylock inspired by a local production of *The Merchant of Venice;* in it he ably defended Shakespeare against the charge of anti-Semitism.[17] Thereafter he wrote no more about Jews nor gave his characters recognizably Jewish surnames. But were these characters in fact Jews in disguise? Here we come to the subtler aspect of the question of Svevo's Jewishness—the extent to which his novels were cryptic-Hebraic in theme and tonality.

The critic Giacomo Debenedetti, himself a Jew, in a major essay published the year after Svevo's death, gave an affirmative answer that has remained the *locus classicus* of the debate. For Debenedetti, the author of *Zeno* had missed a historic opportunity in refusing to serve as "the artist of a certain moment of the Semitic soul"—the moment "when the Jews of Western Europe, emancipated" and "in a lively exchange of sentiment and culture" with the peoples among whom they dwelt, came to "self-consciousness," to a consciousness of their "own difficult values" and the "harsh limits" they were up against. Instead, he had left "the Jewish element . . . obscure" and "the mystery of his own origins . . . in the shadows"; "his Jewish psychology" had "never been explicitly declared." Had Svevo done so, his characters' "expressions" and "words" and "states of mind . . . would have acquired another quality." As Svevo had chosen to depict them, they simply felt an "exasperated" sense of being tarnished—with "a blemish, which, like all blemishes," was " in part congenital and not their responsibility," but from which they suffered and for which they reproached themselves precisely as though they were guilty of something, they knew not what, which demanded expiation. "With an implacability, a taste for vengeance, recalling the passionate ferocity of the Semitic anti-Semite," Svevo "led his protagonist to defeat, without granting him respite, yet at the same time accompanied him in sensual pain, touchy and ready to spring to his defense as with an innate racial solidarity."[18]

A curious passage. The "Semitic anti-Semite" on whose theories Debenedetti drew was none other than Otto Weininger, a dangerously eccentric disciple of Freud, familiar to knowledgeable Triestini such as Svevo. The "Jewish psychology" Debenedetti attributed to Svevo was nothing more nor less than what Weininger characterized as a "feminine" passivity suffused with self-hatred. On the surface the argument sounds plausible enough. Svevo's protagonists, in common with their creator, share a passive posture, all the while thinking of themselves as older and more decrepit than they actually are. They are inept, accident-prone; they mismanage their lives; they envy friends who seem healthier and more self-confident.

All this is only the negative of the portrait. It fits Svevo's earlier novels better than it does the work of his old age. It may be applied to Emilio Brentani, the protagonist of what many prefer as Svevo's most carefully crafted book, *As a Man Grows Older,* but not to Zeno Cosini. With the novel that brought him fame Svevo cunningly shifted his own stance. When he reached the point of *senilità* he had prematurely ascribed to himself and his fictional character alike, he underwent an unexpected rejuvenation. His earlier passivity remained, but the self-denigration which accompanied it took on a more cheerful tone. By the same token, it became more authentically Jewish. The central paradox we need to bear in mind in assessing the relation of Svevo's writing to Judaism is that just at the point he was shaking himself loose from Weininger's sterotype, his half-obliterated heritage began to come clear and to take on positive outlines.

Thus, while Debenedetti was unquestionably right in

detecting a hidden Jewish thread running through Svevo's novels, he caught hold of the wrong strands. He made the whole matter of covert Jewishness more damaging and self-tormenting than it needed to be. It was not true that Svevo invariably "led his protagonist to defeat." Rather, by the time he was ready to compose his Zeno Cosini, who was far more himself than Emilio Brentani had been, he had learned to convert defeat into an ironical kind of victory.

At the age of thirty, Zeno, like his predecessor Emilio, feels himself to be *un uomo finito.* He suffers from obscure maladies; he never succeeds in his constantly announced goal of smoking his "last cigarette"; he works (if such his desultory attempts to make himself useful may be called) in the shadow of his handsome, talented brother-in-law; he suffers from the traumatic memory of his father's having slapped him just before dropping dead; his venture into psychoanalysis turns to farce. His life is punctuated by farcical contretemps: after proposing in vain to two attractive sisters, through a bizarre series of accidents he marries an unprepossessing third; he misses a crucial family funeral by inadvertently joining a procession to another cemetery; when Italy enters the First World War, he is caught on the wrong side of the lines. One could extend the list further. But the point has already emerged: what starts off as tragedy ends as farce—even the father's slap, which remains dreadful only because Zeno has been denied the opportunity to declare his "innocence."

What is more, Zeno's repeated mistakes are reversed over time: the young woman he never intended to marry proves to be precisely the understanding wife he needs; in the supreme crisis of business failure, he demonstrates more acumen and resolution than does his envied brother-in-law. He also outlives his rival: under his apparent hypochondria, he is in fact the more resilient, the healthier, of the two. For in the course of decades of domestic life Zeno has arrived at his own peculiar definition of health, a definition compounded of "indulgence" for his maladies (real or presumed) and his "vices" (such as smoking and marital infidelity) and of a recognition in himself of "benevolence" and even a special form of "latent greatness."[19]

If, then, we are to view Zeno as a crypto-Jew, it is as a Jew with a style of humor familiar to us all from countless folk anecdotes. It is as the ostensibly self-denigrating Jew who in the stories he tells on himself invariably manages to come out on top. It is a person who at bottom knows how to love himself and to be good to himself.[20] And it is a person not without hope.

If this be true, can we go on to say that the undertone of "discomfort" and premature aging eventually vanished from Svevo's life and writings? By no means. He simply managed to raise it to a plane of consciousness on which it became tolerable and on which life itself from time to time could be experienced as enjoyable. The personal and literary achievement—and in view of Svevo's starting point the achievement was monumental—remained nuanced, ambivalent, and hedged with doubt. It was of a piece with his attitude toward Freud and psychoanalysis: at first attraction, then rejection, and in the end a distant, ironical ambivalence.[21]

Although Svevo, in step with his creation Zeno Cosini, at long last learned to derive some pleasure from the process of living, that process (aside from domestic contentment) never acquired much meaning for him. It languished in futility: to be alive was as futile as it was to be a Jew; with both one could do little better than to make them bearable by an occasional wry joke. Hence a certain dryness and an absence of lyricism in Svevo's writing: his attachment to his native city was palpable, but it rose to lyric heights only on the two occasions when Zeno could view it by moonlight from a fishing-boat in the harbor. In Bassani's Ferrara it was to be quite otherwise: such privileged moments were to figure constantly as the stuff of daily experience. But even Bassani, in common with so many Jews before and after him, was to suffer from a sense of being older than he actually was, from a sense of what Svevo called *senilità. Senilità* epitomized the curse that lingered after the sting had been drawn from the recollection of Jewishness. Likewise it was to torment a novelist who lacked any such fund of memory: Alberto Moravia, defrauded by illness of his adolescence, had no choice but to reach for the fruit of precocious knowledge.

Alberto Moravia's World-Weary Adolescents

In 1929, just a year after Svevo's death, the first novel by another unknown and even less recognizably Jewish writer vaulted to equally unanticipated public favor. Once again the author had been obliged to pay for its publication—or in this case, the author's father, since Moravia was only twenty-one and had no money of his own. The success the young man achieved was more of scandal than of esteem: most readers took *The Time of Indifference* to be a sensational, pornographic unmasking of the egoism and heartlessness of Rome's upper bourgeoisie; only gradually did they begin to see that its author, despite his weakness for *coups de théâtre* and the apparent effortlessness of his writing, was in fact a scrupulous craftsman who deserved the fame he was to enjoy for more than a half-century.

In Moravia's case, as opposed to Svevo's, the question of whether he was or was not a Jew scarcely touched the decisive years of his adolescence. Not until his mid-thirties—until the German occupation of Rome in September 1943—did he "know terror," the terror which tens of thousands of his origin had already experienced for a full decade. And even then, a friend's warning that his name figured on a list of those scheduled for deportation and that he had better go into hiding right away, was ambigous: which weighed more heavily in the count against him, his anti-Fascist sentiments or the fact that under a "racial" definition he could be reckoned a Jew?[22]

Moravia himself was not above speaking of a racial atavism in his own family. With his father of Jewish descent, and his mother of Dalmatian Slavic, he described his personality as the product of a "curious amalgam" which had "determined" in him "an excess of sensitivity." One gathers that the Jewish heritage bore the primary blame for this excess: his father's family, he explained, had included "many madmen," a "pathological frequency" which could perhaps be ascribed to the series of "traumas" those of their faith had undergone in both the past and the present. However that might be, Moravia's father was an atheist who had passed on to him "almost nothing" of the Jewish religious tradition. Nor, apparently, had the influence of his mother's Catholicism extended much beyond the formal act of baptism which made him technically a Christian. In everything that counted, the young Alberto grew up without religion.[23]

One might close the discussion there. But at least one should add that the pseudonym he used from *The Time of*

Indifference on suggested no effort to disguise his antecedents. On the contrary, it emphasized one side of them: the surname of an uncle which he chose was as recognizably Jewish as his real name of Pincherle. Unlike Svevo, he did not try to express in it a new identity he had forged.

The "excess of sensitivity" also cries out for comment. If Moravia himself found something Jewish in it, it deserves investigation. The simple fact of the matter—the dominant reality—was that Moravia underwent an inordinately painful adolescence: between the ages of nine and seventeen, he suffered from a tuberculosis of the bone which kept him flat on his back for months at a time, first in a plaster cast, then in traction. Isolated in an Alpine sanatorium, lonely and homesick, he read voraciously and brooded on the fate of European civilization, discovering in it a "social decomposition" which manifested itself in a "highly violent eroticism."[24] The explosion of sex was to be his hallmark as a writer; if anything, it became more pronounced as he grew older. Is it too fanciful to suppose that his obsession derived at least in part from the unpropitious circumstances in which he came to a tormented awareness of his own sexuality? He himself implied as much in an early short story he entitled "Inverno di malato," "A Sick Boy's Winter."[25]

Beyond that, and here we reach the deeper emotional significance of the adolescent concatenation of illness and the awakening of desire, he was convinced of his own malady's psychosomatic origin. Not yet in his teens, he precociously "went through . . . a genuine existential crisis brought on by a great distaste for living." He "fell sick" because he "no longer wanted to live." His cosmic disgust was accompanied by a further conviction of "the impossibility of taking action"—that is, "the problem of action" in the sense of "contact with reality," a problem which, he declared, was to become "the central theme" of all his books and of his life itself.[26]

From time to time Moravia would venture to depict a character capable of self-assertion. By and large, however, his male protagonists remained as passive as Svevo's. By the same token, he was condemned to repeat himself, to write a new version of his first novel again and again. After four decades of reiterating his obsessive theme, he felt at the end of his tether. Into *La noia,* which he published in his early fifties, he poured "the result of all" his "previous experiences." Having set down the story of a man who had exhausted his human potentialities, who had reached the point of stalemate in "all aspects of his personality," Moravia confessed that if he had been "logical" with himself, he would have "written no more."[27] Such was the lugubrious temptation—to which Svevo had nearly succumbed—attendant on an ingrained conviction of *senilità.*

When, in the autumn of 1925, just a few weeks before he turned eighteen, Moravia began to write *The Time of Indifference,* Svevo (who was old enough to be his grandfather) was still alive. At the time, the fledgling novelist had not yet read *Zeno,* and he was to deny any influence of his great predecessor on his own work. Yet he came to admire Svevo and to rank him along with Manzoni as one of the two "real novelists" his country had produced. In Svevo, Moravia detected an "elegance" and "grace" which he himself lacked and, in the absence of these qualities, no "points of contact" between them.[28] It was of course by sheer accident (or a remote kinship?) that the younger man had settled on a pen name which recalled the elder writer's ancestry and marriage. Whatever elective affinity Moravia's readers might later discern had nothing to do with style or artistic conception; it had to do with a shared sense of futility.

Although conceived without inspiration from *As a Man Grows Older, The Time of Indifference* echoed its themes in uncanny fashion: a brother and a sister with their emotional fortunes closely intertwined; the sister succumbing to the "animal" egoism of a thoughtless, self-confident man; the brother, as a passive spectator of this desolation, languishing in a conviction of the weakness of his own character. In both cases the brother is depicted as a dreamer attempting without avail to reconstruct the reality about him to conform with his dimly understood longings—to discover in imagination or in the flesh the ideal woman he craves. Hence with both a flabby species of "purity" sets them apart from the worldliness of others. Alike prone to melancholy, Svevo's Emilio is the more contemplative, Moravia's Michele the more anguished. But they share a sense that life is over before it has fully begun and that it is beyond their powers to make a new start. Both novels close on the note of a *vita nuova* as impossible to attain.[29]

One obvious difference needs underlining: Svevo's prematurely old protagonist is in his thirties, Moravia's still under twenty. The disabused Roman seemed unable to let go the theme of adolescent despair. Twice more, in short novels that rank among his most celebrated, he returned to the obsession which haunted him: his Agostino, at thirteen, was to experience a precocious desperation in the deceptively cheerful setting of a summer resort; his Luca, two years older, was to go through a more profound emotional crisis in his native city. The first story appeared in 1944, the second in 1948. But both had been conceived and largely composed years earlier. It is curious to note that just as Luca has been described as an Agostino back home from the beach, so Dino, the protagonist of *La noia* and the final figure in the succession, was, as a man in his mid-thirties, and after the lapse of nearly two decades in his creator's life, to be of the age the two boys would have reached had Moravia pursued their fortunes further.

Agostino and *Luca* were less convincing than *The Time of Indifference.* As opposed to the unmistakable authenticity of Moravia's first novel, they bore the marks of an over-hasty or undigested reading of Freud—more particularly the latter, tracing, as it did, "a psychological crisis according to a predetermined *schema.*"[30] The pubescent Agostino is as yet scarcely conscious of his erotic yearning: he suffers from the homosexual innuendoes of age-mates of a lower social order and greater worldly wisdom than his; simultaneously, and with redoubled torment after being turned away from a house of prostitution as too young to lose his virginity, he little by little perceives the ambivalence tinged with sexuality in his feelings for his own mother. Agostino begins his sunlit adventures as a seaside idyll; he ends them with the prospect of the "years and years of emptiness and frustration" that lie ahead before the adolescent can become a man.[31]

In contrast, Luca at fifteen is quite aware of his sexual desires. But they bring him no joy—no more than anything else in his comfortable upper-bourgeois existence. His is the story of a boy whose "revolt against the world" has assumed "the characteristics of a strike." "Conscious . . . of a mournful feeling" like that of an "animal, ill-adapted for life, slinking back to its lair to die in peace," he concludes that he "must disobey" his parents and his teachers, that he must commit what he does not yet recognize as "a kind of suicide" in the form of "a ritual sacrifice." And in so doing he manages to fall seriously ill. On the brink of the death he only half intended, he finds salvation in the overripe woman who nurses him back to health. This time the adolescent's virginity triumphantly succumbs; in the arms of his "second and truer mother," he experiences a "second birth." And one epiphany is followed by another. On his way to convalescence in a mountain sanatorium, the sight of "a snow-covered peak" looming up before him fills Luca with a "trustful, drunken exultation."[32]

"So trustful a Moravia will not be found again"—such is the verdict of his most learned psychoanalytic critic, who adds a transposition of Descartes' classic maxim in the form of *"coito, ergo sum."*[33] Unquestionably Luca's despair and his sickness alike echoed his creator's own boyhood experience. The same could well be true of sexual initiation. One might hazard the guess that some comparable outpouring of physical and emotional release occurred to Moravia himself in the brief interval between his discharge from his own sanatorium and his sitting down to write his first novel. And it may have been in the succeeding period of living alone in one mountain hotel after another that he settled into his bedrock conviction about the supreme potency of sexual consummation—which could occasionally be redemptive, as in the case of Luca, but more often figured in brutal fashion as a relentless urgency.

It is not hard to convince a man enslaved by his own sexuality of the futility of living. From there it is only a step to world-weariness—and beyond that, to a hatred of oneself. Perhaps this was what Moravia had in mind when he hinted at something Jewish in his "excess of sensitivity." The paradox of the matter would seem to be that Svevo, who recognized his Jewishness, eventually struggled his way loose from self-torment, while Moravia, who scarcely thought of himself as Jewish at all, never succeeded in overcoming it. His protagonists lingered behind Svevo's Zeno in the shallows of despair: despising themselves, they clutched at sexuality as the only form of salvation they knew. By the same token, Moravia's baleful example was to loom over writers of Jewish origin younger than he—both as a model of professional dedication and plain speaking about subjects on which others kept silent and as a warning of the slough of despond into which a shared "excess of sensitivity" might entice them.[34]

Two readings of Dante may serve to epitomize a crucial change in emotional tone.[35] The first is from Moravia's *Luca.* Already shivering with fever, the boy, called upon to read aloud in class, barely manages to get through the narrative of Bonconte of Montefeltro, fallen in battle, whose corpse is swallowed up by the ice-cold waters of the swollen Arno. Luca pauses in anguish not only because he is ill; he chokes with emotion at the recognition of his emotional affinity with what he is reading, at his sense that he is in effect declaiming his own story. The same is true of Primo Levi's fragmentary recitation (for this time no text is at hand) of the legendary last voyage of Ulysses, in the modern inferno of a concentration camp. Levi too discovers an affinity with his own condition: in the Greek king's desperate venture of sailing out into the uncharted and forbidden ocean beyond the Pillars of Hercules, he glimpses a paradigm of the human extremity that he himself and his fellow-prisoners have reached.

There the resemblance ends. The pampered offspring of the rich can discern nothing but desolation in the fate of Bonconte. Ulysses and his companions perish also: they too go down to a watery grave. But the wretched inmate of a living hell finds meaning in their death: although much else in Dante's passage slips his mind, he remembers the words with which Ulysses exhorts his companions to follow him to the ends of the earth:

> fatti non foste a viver come bruti,
> ma per seguir virtute e conoscenza.

They were not "made . . . to live like brute beasts"—though this is in fact how Levi and his interlocutor are living—"but to pursue virtue and knowledge." And perhaps that is precisely what those who have been deprived of their humanity can still manage to strive for: all at once Levi perceives "something gigantic," the reason for his sufferings, in the notion that it is on an ultimate voyage beyond the limits of the human that he has embarked.

A final paradox indeed. A new lyricism was to appear at the most unlikely time, in the holocaust generation of writers—in three figures, almost of an age, who were to experience in their own persons the scourge of persecution, plus the eternally youthful Carlo Levi, a half generation older than they, who shared their perils and their sensibility. The new tone was both tender and ironic—the new vision was suffused with the tranquil light of a tremulous serenity, as though seen through a veil. To writers such as these, harsh words of denunciation came only as a last resort: the dominant note was one of fraternity and of hope.

3

Two Captives Called Levi

In Italy, as elsewhere in Europe, the Hitler era drew a deep gash through contemporary Jewish history. At the same time, as always in the Italian experience, equally profound differences distinguished the vicissitudes of the peninsula's Jews from the lot of the majority of their coreligionists. For one thing, their country had been Fascist for a decade before Nazism came to power; indeed, Hitler and his henchmen regarded Mussolini's movement as the precursor of their own. For another, in view of the apparent eclipse of Italian anti-Semitism in the preceding quarter-century, the official adoption of such a policy descended with the cruel force of an unanticipated catastrophe. Moreover, it came in two phases: first, in the autumn of 1938, on the Duce's own initiative; five years later, with the wartime German occupation, as an extension of the Nazi program of uprooting and mass murder. A final point of difference: a higher percentage of Italy's Jews survived the terror than was true of any other major country under German rule.

Fascism and Italian Jewry

At the start there was nothing anti-Semitic about the Fascist regime. There were to be sure anti-Semites among the extremists in the movement, but for its first decade and a half of power, these never set the dominant tone. All too eager to be reassured, Italy's Jews answered Mussolini's call: the number of them who signed up as Fascists of the first hour proved once again, as in other fields of endeavor, disproportionately high. Lest this statement sound disparaging, one should hasten to add that philo-Fascism among Italian Jewry was only natural: Mussolini's movement was both patriotic and predominantly middle class; so were the Jews. Further qualifications spring to mind. A distinguished minority of the early enthusiasts—notably the Milanese lawyer and writer Eucardio Momigliano—soon repented their decision and swung over to the opposing side. And that opposition, as it grew in size, particularly among intellectuals, once more found a disproportionately large share of Jews in its ranks. True to a long-standing tradition of commitment, Italy's Jews tended to opt either for the ruling ideology or for explicit anti-Fascism and were less likely than the majority of their countrymen to shrug their shoulders and avoid making a choice. Such a polarization of opinion was reflected in the contrasting attitudes that prevailed in individual communities: if Ferrara's Jewish elite had a deserved reputation for militant Fascism, Turin's eventually fell under official suspicion as a hotbed of dissent. The greatest of Jewish oppositionists, however, came from Tuscany—Carlo Rosselli, linked by ties of kinship with the Nathan and Pincherle families of Rome, the organizer of the most dynamic wing of anti-Fascism in exile, who was slaughtered with his brother Nello by French fascists in

Mussolini's pay a year before the Duce took the anti-Semitic plunge.[1]

What of Mussolini himself? On this subject the Duce's own statements were so contradictory and interpretations of them have diverged so widely that historians might well be tempted to throw up their hands in despair. Careful scrutiny, however, has detected a guiding thread through the tangle of inconsistencies: Mussolini never shared the conventional (or "establishment") attitude that the Jews should be regarded as indistinguishable from other Italians. Still more, his relations with individual Jews were freighted with emotion and frequently ambivalent. At one time, he would overrate the strength of Judaism; at another, he would disparage it. He oscillated between "extravagantly philo-Semitic" pronouncements—the last one as late as 1935—and incoherent mutterings against "international Jewry." He both respected and feared the power of Jewish high finance; he distrusted Zionism as potentially disruptive of national unity, while favoring it as a weapon against British pretensions in the eastern Mediterranean. Back in the days when he had been a Socialist, the Jewish leader Claudio Treves had figured as perhaps his chief antagonist within the party—their enmity leading to a duel in 1915. Two of Mussolini's mistresses were Jewish—one of them his biographer—and both received shabby treatment at his hands.[2] However one sifts the evidence, it seems clear that for Mussolini, Jews were no ordinary people: he could love or hate them, admire or revile them, but he never managed, as so many of his countrymen did, to take them for granted.

Hence after his alignment with Hitler in 1936, it was only to be expected that he would eventually feel obliged to sort out his contradictory attitudes. He took two years to do so.

When in the autumn of 1938 the Grand Council of Fascism promulgated a declaration which echoed the Nuremberg Laws in the drastic limitations it placed on the rights of Jews to contract mixed marriages, to teach or to study, and to hold jobs and property, most people assumed that Mussolini was merely doing what Hitler told him. The truth was more complex.

Three distinctions, at the very least, need to be made. First, no *direct* German pressure forced the Duce's hand; he acted on his own.[3] Second, he made an elaborate, if ultimately futile, effort to fabricate an indigenous Italian brand of anti-Semitism. Conscious of its lack of resonance among his own people (and of the fact that German racists despised the Italians as swarthy Mediterraneans), he eschewed biological or anthropological pseudo-science and based his arguments on "creative" or "spiritualist" considerations. Finally, he never intended the physical extermination of the Jews. He simply wished to push them out of the mainstream of Italian life and, if possible, out of Italy altogether.[4] To this latter end his government facilitated the departure not only of native-born Jews but of the German nationals who during the previous half-decade had been fleeing over the Alps to what they quite understandably regarded as a safe haven.

None of the above should be taken—as it sometimes has been—as exonerating Mussolini; it is meant merely to demonstrate once more that he was no monster on the scale of a Hitler or a Stalin. Obviously such reflections, whether offered at the time or subsequently, would bring cold comfort to the Italian Jews. The victims were stunned and incredulous at what had befallen them. Most had tried to deny the mounting evidence that Mussolini was about to change course: they had failed to heed the press campaign against them which for the two previous years had been gaining in intensity, the "Manifesto of the Race" published in July by an undistinguished set of Fascist "intellectuals," the provisions excluding Jews from institutions of learning which had come a month before the Grand Council's global decision. They could not believe what was happening: they had felt too secure; they had been reassured too often.

When at length the last illusions were stripped away, Italy's Jews succumbed to a bitter sense of betrayal, sometimes coupled with the feelings of shame or guilt, "they knew not for what," that Debenedetti had ascribed to them. After all, they had been "good Italians," better than most, and this was their reward. More particularly they grieved that the King had let them down. His father and his grandfather (and he himself in his younger days) had stood loyally by the Jews at a time when Europe's other royal houses kept them at a distance. Now Victor Emmanuel III was limiting himself to a "timid resistance" which in the end was reduced to a "platonic invitation to recognize the merits of those who had distinguished themselves by their patriotism." Nor was much to be expected of the Pope. Pius XI opposed the anti-Semitic legislation on "one point alone: that of the marriages of converted Jews." He seemed far more concerned about the prerogatives of the Church than about the fate of the Jews themselves.[5] It would require a genuine reign of terror to shake his successor into a firmer stand.

❧

So the Jews settled as best they could into a situation of barely tolerated marginality. Among the educated classes men who had overnight lost positions of respect and influence shut themselves up at home in mournful seclusion. Their sons went abroad to study. Those who in return for past services enjoyed the privilege of "discrimination" (the word in Italian having just the opposite of its meaning in English) fared better than the majority of their coreligionists. Besides these, there were more than 4,000 who tried to improve their lot through baptism—"new Marranos," a "source of grave embarrassment to the Catholic hierarchy as well as . . . of friction between Church and State."[6] For nearly five years the Jews of Italy lived in a bizarre twilight zone, prey to unremitting anxiety, uncertain of the future, at the mercy of the whims of an officialdom that sometimes enforced the full rigor of the law, more often tempered it with humanity. Even after Mussolini's declaration of war alongside Hitler in June 1940 the situation of Italian Jewry remained unclear: the surreal atmosphere of the era may be suggested by recalling that foreign Jews were still finding refuge in the peninsula and that, in the first seven months of the country's belligerency, 2,000 succeeded in taking ship for Palestine or other points of safety.[7]

The half-decade of mitigated persecution came to an abrupt end in September 1943. With the armistice of that month and the German military occupation which followed, there began the second and infinitely more brutal phase of Italian Jewry's sufferings. Fortunately it was short—just over a year and a half. But its brevity was outbalanced by the tragic accident of the way the country was divided in two. Only a handful of Jews could profit from the liberation the Anglo-American invaders were bringing to the South; in the Center and North, where the bulk of Italy's Jews lived, the Nazis were both conducting a tenacious delaying action, as they retreated step by step up the peninsula, and imposing their meticulously sadistic version of anti-Semitic orthodoxy.

In these drastically altered circumstances Mussolini lost

control of his own policy. Reduced to the humiliating role of a German puppet, he was no longer in a position to apply his peculiar notions of how Jews should be handled. The "moderate" decrees of his neo-Fascist government on the subject remained a dead letter. But at least he refrained from cooperating fully with the Nazi program of extermination. He continued to play a double game, as he had earlier done in the areas of France and the Balkans under Italian occupation, in theory professing a strident anti-Semitism, in practice looking the other way when subordinates protected threatened Jewish groups or individuals. In this respect the record of his regime contrasts favorably with that of Marshal Pétain in Vichy, which virtually volunteered its services to the Gestapo.[8] What can be charged against Mussolini—and it is a serious charge indeed—is that he pursued a course which proved thoroughly unrealistic and counterproductive. With the apparent intention of postponing the solution of the "Jewish question" until the war's end, in late November 1943 his government ordered a general internment for the duration. This order, "though designed to protect the Jews, had the effect of facilitating" their extermination. If the majority went into hiding, a substantial number—for one last time too trustful—followed instructions that put them at the mercy of Nazi executioners assisted by local neo-Fascist zealots. The best one can say of Mussolini's actions is that, although he "was too much of an Italian to approve of the 'final solution,' . . . he and his henchmen helped to create the conditions in which the Holocaust became possible."[9]

Six weeks before the internment order the Gestapo had swooped down upon the Jews of Rome, rounding up more than a thousand for deportation to Auschwitz. The Sabbath night of October 15-16, 1943, inaugurated the systematic pursuit of Italian Jewry that was to continue for the next eighteen months. It also tried the conscience of Pius XII, who had been elevated to the papal throne in early 1939. The much-vexed question of what the Pope did or failed to do extends far beyond the limits of the present study. Suffice it to say that for Italy at any rate his case needs to be treated in at least as nuanced a fashion as Mussolini's. In the autumn of 1943, as on so many previous and subsequent occasions, Pius XII failed to speak out; his expression of concern went no farther than a brief declaration by the Vatican newspaper that his "universal and paternal succor" knew "no bounds of nationality, religion *or race.*"[10] At the same time, he offered sanctuary in Vatican City and its dependent ecclesiastical establishments to those in danger, and he let it be known that he trusted his example would be followed beyond the limits of Rome—to what good effect has already been observed.

Despite the Duce's lukewarmness and the Pope's carefully circumscribed effort to save lives, the Nazi terror raged unchecked. One can scarcely list even the major acts of brutality which turned the year 1944 and the early months of 1945 into a nightmare surpassing the Italian Jews' worst imaginings. A few episodes, however, deserve to be commemorated: the massacre of nearly fifty Jews in the summer resorts around Lake Maggiore; the slaughter of seventy-eight Jewish hostages in the Ardeatine Caves near Rome; the shooting down of Giuseppe Pardo Roques, the universally respected president of the Pisan Jewish community. Only a small fraction of the victims, however, perished on Italian soil; the vast majority—about 7,500—died in extermination camps, from which fewer than 1,000 returned.

At the war's end the number of Jews living in Italy, which the arrival of foreigners had swelled to approximately 45,000, had been halved. But of those lost to Italy, nearly three-fifths (perhaps as many as 9,000) had succeeded in emigrating. Of the more than 36,000 obliged or choosing to stay, just under four-fifths had been saved. What had made possible this apparent miracle, surpassed only by the record of Denmark?[11]

The physical and linguistic "indistinguishability" of the Italian Jews had of course helped them mightily in eluding their pursuers. Far more important was the attitude of the Italian people. It is not going too far to state that from the start they had sabotaged the anti-Semitism decreed from above. By the time this policy gave way to mass destruction, men and women who earlier had limited themselves to small acts of kindliness became willing to run risks on behalf of the Jews. Countless tales of spontaneous hospitality—characteristically by peasants and small folk—shine on in the memories of the survivors. As early as the great roundup in Rome, a Gestapo report described the "behavior of the Italian people" as "outright passive resistance which in many individual cases amounted to active assistance."[12] Nearly all the Jews who came through the war alive owed their survival to the neighbors—or utter strangers—who gave them shelter. The lengths to which such aid might go is suggested by the story of a bishop who smuggled a Jewish woman out of his Piedmontese city by concealing her in a coffin and providing her with a funeral escort! The anecdote also illustrates the key role in the work of salvation played by members of the Catholic clergy—from high ecclesiastics to simple monks and nuns and parish priests—who in this supreme trial of their faith and fortitude proved themselves "truly Christians."[13]

Before the horror ended—in April 1945, with the liberation of the North and the collapse of the neo-Fascist republic—the members of Italy's Jewish communities had scattered in a thousand directions. Most of course had tried to lie low, preferably in areas where they would not be recognized. Scores of intellectuals had gone into exile, where a number remained, having found a welcome in their new homes in Palestine or Britain or the United States. (One may think of such distinguished figures on the MIT faculty as the historian of science Giorgio de Santillana, the virologist Salvador Luria, the economist Franco Modigliani, and the physicist Bruno Rossi.)[14] Between two and three thousand had joined the armed Resistance—once again a number out of all proportion to the Jewish percentage of the Italian population. Two in particular were destined for leadership in the postwar Communist party: Umberto Terracini, Antonio Gramsci's friend and coworker and the veteran of a decade and a half of Fascist imprisonment, and Emilio Sereni, who was to apply Gramsci's theoretical structure to the study of the Italian countryside. Emilio Sereni was the younger brother of the Enzo we have already encountered as a militant Zionist. Enzo too, back from Palestine, where he had become the acknowledged chief of the Italians in the kibbutzim, threw himself into the Resistance with his characteristic energy and disdain for personal safety. Parachuted into the North, he was captured by the Germans and slain at Dachau in November 1944.[15]

Such varied experiences, whether tragic or touched with the warmth of a common humanity, were to provide the material for a rich literature of recollection. The shock of persecution stimulated in Italy, as it did elsewhere, the reawakening of a dormant Jewish consciousness. But just as among the Italian Jews this shock came with redoubled force because they had felt themselves little different from their neighbors, so its literary repercussions resonated on a corresponding level of universality. When an Italian Jew wrote of the sufferings he or she had endured, it was not simply *as a Jew:* it was as someone giving testimony on behalf of all the victims of oppression, wherever and of whatever religious origin they might be.

The Physician-Painter Don Carlo: Exile and Wonder-Worker

Carlo Levi, born in Turin in 1902, was five years older than Moravia; they were alike of the fully assimilated generation which grew up in the period between the waning of the old religiously based anti-Semitism and the advent of the new "racial" variety. No more than Moravia's was his youth colored by Jewish associations. Yet his ancestry was Jewish on both sides, and the accidents of his existence threw him into closer contact with Jews than was true of the Roman novelist. Moreover, he made a far deeper ideological commitment. With his advanced degree in medicine—a profession he scarcely practiced—he became successively (and on occasion simultaneously) a painter, a writer, and a political activist. All of which may suggest how he plunged into his varied doings with a zest and volubility that were quite foreign to the taciturn, gloomy, self-doubting Moravia. Carlo Levi radiated joy in the process of living; wherever he went, he brought a festive atmosphere with him.

In the absence of Judaism, politics permeated his childhood. As a boy he made the acquaintance of the "general staff" of Italian Socialism in the guise of family friends; his mother was the sister of Mussolini's old enemy Claudio Treves. He knew Gramsci; he knew the patriarch of Italian Socialism, Filippo Turati. But his first close friend and political associate was neither Jewish nor Socialist. It was a young man of his own age named Piero Gobetti, the *wunderkind* of an unconventional and explosive variety of liberalism, who founded his first political and cultural review when only seventeen and died at the age of twenty-five as a result of Fascist beatings. Carlo Levi never ceased mourning for Gobetti. No one could quite replace him, not even Levi's second ideological mentor and inspirer, who was none other than Carlo Rosselli, the gadfly of the anti-Fascists who had fled to France. It was in large part to see Rosselli that at the end of the 1920's Levi acquired the habit of making frequent trips to Paris. From these visits he returned prepared to serve as the chief Piedmontese organizer for Rosselli's movement, *Giustizia e Libertà.*[16]

In his ideological efforts he was seconded by a younger friend, Leone Ginzburg, the future husband of the writer Natalia. With Rosselli and Ginzburg, and the circle of Torinese youth who followed their lead, Levi found himself at last in an *ambiente* which was predominantly of Jewish origin. But the fact that his associates were Jews seems to have affected him only marginally: it was their politics rather than their antecedents that bound them together; not until four decades later was Natalia Ginzburg to write of a "secret complicity" which linked one Italian Jew to another. In the meantime, Carlo Levi barely mentioned them. His first major book, *Christ Stopped at Eboli,* was devoid of Jewish characters—quite understandably so, in view of its southern peasant setting. His second, *The Watch,* introduced two Jews as minor, episodic figures. Both were from the Roman plebs, both victims of the frightful Nazi roundup of mid-October

1943—one a woman half-crazed by the loss of her husband and her son, the other a concentration-camp survivor, obsessed with a frantic and perverse admiration of German efficiency—in short, both grotesques. Levi depicted them from the outside, as a painter on the prowl for the picturesque; even toward the bereaved wife and mother he scarcely betrayed his never-failing human sympathy.[17] It was as though he lacked any point of contact with such as these, or perhaps they recalled in a manner too close for comfort the ghetto existence which Jews of his class thought they had long ago left behind.

Whatever residual Jewish consciousness Carlo Levi harbored he expressed indirectly through his boundless admiration for his older friend Saba, whom he ranked as modern Italy's greatest poet. They first met in the mid-1920s at Debenedetti's house; subsequently they were in hiding close to one another in Florence during the German wartime occupation. In Saba, Levi celebrated the half-Jew who had succeeded in transforming the "ancient conflict" within his ancestry, the "tremendous anguish" of his life, into the "most celestial serenity." Although never observant and never willing to recognize a cultural distinction between what was Jewish and what was not, Saba, Levi maintained, wove a "thread" of the Jewish tradition into his writings. His "character . . . was profoundly Jewish, in its capacity to universalize everyday life," and with it the "figures" of ordinary existence, and to give to those figures an "absolute," a "biblical" quality embracing all men in all their days on this earth.[18]

The word "biblical" prompts a final reflection on the ancestral residue in Carlo Levi's consciousness. Deep within he cherished a religious sensibility that Svevo and Moravia lacked. He read his Bible—curiously enough in a Protestant rather than Jewish version. It was one of two or three books he took with him during a nomadic existence in which he necessarily traveled light. It provides an initial key to the universality of sympathy that he found in Saba and that was to flower in the wretched soil of the Italian South.

With his talent for converting disaster into a blessing, Carlo Levi extracted from the boredom and loneliness of ten months of enforced residence the materials for a masterpiece of amateur anthropology. Arrested first in 1934 and again the following year, this second time he was shipped off to the desolate, stony and almost treeless region known earlier as the Basilicata, subsequently as Lucania. It was of course as an anti-Fascist rather than as a Jew that he was punished; Mussolini's anti-Semitic legislation was still three years away. And the comparative mildness of his sentence, the fact that he was free to move about and live as he chose within the immediate surroundings of the village to which he was confined, may underscore once more the distinction between Fascist and Nazi practice. Even his release came earlier than expected: though totally devoid of martial or imperial enthusiasms, he profited from the amnesty decreed to celebrate Italy's conquest of Ethiopia.

The better part of a decade went by before he put pen to paper to tell what he had learned from the peasants of the South. And by that time his sufferings of the mid-1930s must have figured in recollection as mere child's play. (Moreover, it was not his own misery which concerned him, but that of the people among whom he had been obliged to dwell.) Meanwhile he had gone into exile in France; he had been caught up in the great retreat of 1940; he had returned to Italy and been arrested still a third time. From this last confinement he was rescued by Mussolini's fall in the summer of 1943—a happy event canceled out a month and a half later by the dreaded descent of the Germans. Finally bowing to the dictates of elementary prudence, Carlo Levi went into hiding. From December to the following July, until the arrival of the Anglo-American liberators, he sat "closed in one room" in Florence, alone with the memories that little by little took the form of a series of vignettes linked one to another by sustained meditation.

The "world apart" in which he was writing forcibly recalled to him the comparable universe of the southern peasantry, "hedged in by custom and sorrow, cut off from History and the State, eternally patient," in a "land without comfort or solace," a "motionless civilization on barren ground . . . in the presence of death." *Christ Stopped at Eboli,* so the peasants had told him, and so he entitled his book. Eboli, to the north and west, was still a town of "Christians"—that is, in their language, human beings. Jesus had gone that far but no farther. He had never reached the village Levi called Gagliano, where, the peasants explained, they continued to live "as beasts, beasts of burden, or even less than beasts."[19]

However his northern sophistication might set him off from those about him, Carlo Levi soon discovered that he was bound to them by a "passive fraternity" of shared oppression. He and his fellow-*confinati*—or "exiles," as the peasants called them—ranked as "brothers"; they too, for "mysterious reasons," had fallen afoul of the distant, hostile, uncomprehending government in Rome. The sense of being "victims of the . . . same fate" offered an initial path to mutual sympathy.[20] Still more did the prestige Levi enjoyed as a novel variety of a figure long familiar to the regional folkore: the wonder-worker endowed with magical powers, in this case beneficent.

In "Gagliano," unintentionally and reluctantly, he found himself obliged to practice his original profession, which he had almost forgotten. The local physicians were incompetents or charlatans, scorning the peasants, who would turn to them only as a last resort. Levi, in contrast, proved both skilled and humane: with the scantiest armory of medicine and equipment he effected a handful of spectacular cures which the villagers took to be miraculous. Still more: when he was not snatching his neighbors from the jaws of death, he was painting pictures—of landscapes, of children—whose vivid colors likewise seemed to have something magical about them. The peasants, he had early noted, did not sing; in their dark, melancholy lives there was no room for joy. Levi on occasion would sing—and he revealed still another hidden talent when he consented to play the organ in church. Taken together, his marvelous bag of tricks made him a "Christian" of another (and exalted) species to those who little by little learned to love and venerate him. Where they were swarthy and clothed in black and deeply suspicious one of another, he was blond and rosy and overflowing with a bright, spontaneous generosity.

Hence, when by another of the capriciously cruel decrees that made the peasants hate and fear "the people in Rome," Levi was forbidden to practice medicine any longer, revolt threatened; the age-old cry went up: "We'll burn the town hall and kill the mayor." Fortunately no blood was shed. A tacit understanding with the same mayor permitted Levi to continue his work of healing, but discreetly and covertly. The reprieve proved pathetically brief. Scarcely had the villagers recovered from their dismay when they learned of the imminent departure of the wonder-worker who in southern style was now universally greeted as "Don Carlo." This time their desolation knew no bounds. And even he, delighted as he was to be returning to "civilization," could not suppress a pang of regret for the eerie serenity he had at least once experienced among them. Watching through the night, he recalled, in the house of a dying peasant, "lost beyond time, in an infinite elsewhere," he seemed "to have entered . . . into the very heart of the world. An immense happiness" that he had "never felt before . . . filled" him "totally," and with it a "flowing sense of . . . plenitude."[21]

You should stay among us and *fare lo stregone,* practice sorcery—so his housekeeper, who had mastered the arts of witchcraft, had earlier advised. It would be too much to say that Levi was tempted by the prospect; but his account of the incident betrays an ironic satisfaction in having been singled out for such an honor. And in delineating as accurately as he could the role devised for him, he let slip the word *rofe',* Hebrew for healer.[22] Evidently his ignorance of his ancestral heritage was not as total as those who encountered him only casually might suppose.

The notion of healer—Levi's Jewish memory—supplied the warm, living bond to southern peasant actuality. A curious parallel may illuminate this uncanny power. Giuseppe Pardo Roques we have already encountered as the president of the Pisan community, slaughtered in 1944 by the Nazis. Among the Jews of Pisa, Roques bore the honorary title of *parnas,* or leader. Although the victim of crippling phobias, he inspired respect wherever he went, and he was rightly esteemed a man of deep humanity and wisdom. There apparently ran a secret, mysterious link between his own psychic illness and his ability to help others. Consumed by irrational terrors, he had it in his power to give a sense of reassurance and safety to those who had taken refuge in his house until the very moment of their death together. And this death Roques met with steadfastness: when a *real* danger appeared, he knew how to instill courage in his friends and neighbors. He, like Carlo Levi, could perform miracles.[23]

With his book Levi brought about a miracle of another kind. He succeeded in awakening his countrymen, that is, highly educated northerners like himself, to the bitter realities of the Italian South; he managed what three generations of *meridionalisti,* of professional students of the area far more qualified than he, had failed to accomplish. With his painter's eye trained to catch the nuances of human variety, with his physician's hands skilled in probing the wounds of his fellowmen, he was on the alert for the inarticulate, barely voiced sentiments which revealed a way of life at once alien and universal, harsh and grievously afflicted. Where others had lined up the statistics of misery, he went beyond economics to explore a world untouched by the modern spirit, still more, pagan in its worship of earth-divinities and in its total lack of transcendent hope. Levi brought that hope to the peasants among whom he dwelt—and whose plea for a bare minimum of human understanding he carried with him on his departure.

It took more than a decade for Carlo Levi to redeem his promise to return to "Gagliano." By the time he did so, *Christ Stopped at Eboli* had made him a celebrity, a public figure. Nothing he wrote subsequently remotely approached it in literary power or public esteem.

In 1963 he did something that struck many who knew him as both uncharacteristic and quixotic. With a lifetime commitment to democratic Socialism behind him, he agreed to run for the Italian Senate on a Communist-backed ticket, winning a seat in the same godforsaken Lucania to which he had been exiled a generation before. The choice of constituency explains the apparent political apostasy. As *their* senator, Levi could speak for *his* peasants in the halls of power in Rome. What is more, by the time of his election they too were traversing the same experience that he had previously gone through among them: tens of thousands were living abroad as foreign workers. Levi visited them—in Belgium, in Switzerland—to console them in their loneliness and to raise their spirits with his unflagging good humor and sympathy. To a Communist friend he confessed that this kind of activity appealed to him far more than listening to debates in the Senate. The South, he declared, had become his "home." Christ had still to arrive there, but he, Levi, at least, could go in search of his "brothers" forced by the cruel necessity of labor to live far away.[24]

When he died in 1975, Carlo Levi was serving as president of the federation of Italian emigrants. It was a fitting end to the spiritual voyage on which he had embarked four decades earlier.

The Chemist Primo: "Poet" of the Concentration Camp

Before a full-fledged Jew has appeared on the scene, we have already detected two echoes or resonances of familiar Jewish themes. In Svevo and Moravia we found the ingrained sorrow, the weariness of a life not yet lived, epitomized by the conviction of *senilità*. In Carlo Levi there appeared the age-old theme of exile. At the hands of a younger man bearing the same hallowed surname, although bound by no tie of kinship, this theme was to emerge with classic, crystalline purity in a record of sufferings infinitely more grievous than mere banishment to the South. Of the desolate village called Gagliano, Carlo Levi had written with effusive tenderness. Of the inner circle of hell called Auschwitz, Primo Levi wrote in a tone that was equally tender, but with the restraint imposed by the stern necessity of transmuting unprecedented horror into a kind of "poetry" that likewise had no earlier model on which to draw.

With Primo Levi we come at last to a "real" Jew. He too was a Torinese, born in 1919 in the same house on the Corso Re Umberto where he was to raise his own family in the postwar years. He had in common with Carlo Levi an advanced degree in science, in this case chemistry; but unlike the older man, he was to stick to his original profession, with pride, dignity, and independence, throughout his life. For him, the chemist incarnated the eternal struggle to pry open the secrets of the universe; a modern "Moses," he stood awaiting his "law." And the revelation did not disappoint him: the periodic table of the atoms—which decades later was to suggest a title for his autobiography—delighted him with its austere "poetry"; the "strong and bitter taste" of his craft steadied his life against the trials that lay ahead. Still more, to study and to practice the art of chemistry meant a liberation into reality from the rhetorical abstractions of Italian classical education, which when Levi reached adolescence had been cheapened and distorted by Fascist evasiveness, if not downright lying; science, "clear and distinct and . . . verifiable," served as an "antidote to Fascism." A reading of Moravia's *The Time of Indifference* further opened Levi's eyes to the moral squalor about him. By the time he reached manhood he had trained himself to penetrating observation, first of the material, then of the human world; he had become a person whom others trusted with their secrets, a person "to whom many things are told." And when at last he in his turn had a tale to tell, he saw himself as an Ancient Mariner restored by miracle to the company of the living: no inattention could dissuade him from his act of exorcism, from pressing insistently on the "others" the grisly story that few were disposed to hear.[25]

Although Bar Mitzvah at the age of thirteen, Primo Levi, like so many others of his generation, had paid no particular heed to his Jewishness until six years later the anti-Semitic laws hit him just at the moment he was to begin advanced studies. Overnight what had figured as merely "a cheerful little anomaly" between him and his Christian friends became a source of discomfort on both sides. While no one, neither professor nor student, directed any "hostile word or gesture" toward him, he felt that they were keeping their distance, and he responded in kind. Isolated and lonely, cast out as "impure," he "began to be proud" of his impurity. In his need he found a friend in another misfit, a sturdy young man of peasant origin, cut off from the others by class rather than religion. This heaven-sent companion taught the city-bred Levi the technique of rock-climbing: together they sought out perilous slopes, unwittingly hardening themselves for the "iron future" which was coming closer each day. The friend was one of the first to fall in the Partisan struggle.[26]

Meantime Levi faced the problem of continuing his studies in the teeth of legislation that debarred him from the University. After being rebuffed by several professors in lofty or embarrassed fashion, he finally found an unconventional laboratory assistant prepared to circumvent the regulations and take him on—an ironical unbeliever (whether religious or ideological) who answered Levi's anxious query "with two words of the Gospel: 'Follow me.'"[27] Apparently no informer betrayed the irregularity. In 1941 Levi received his doctor's degree *summa cum laude.* By then Italy was at war; the task of finding employment loomed as insuperable. For two years Levi lived by odd jobs—in a nickel mine, in a varnish factory—until at length he reached Milan.

Here the ultimate discovery awaited him. In the city that ranked for both friend and foe of the regime as the "moral capital of Italy," he learned of the existence of militant anti-Fascism. As a boy in Turin he had known "almost nothing" of Carlo Levi and his circle of conspirators, broken up by imprisonment and exile. The slender thread of dissent never reached that far. Now he found himself obliged to begin his anti-Fascist education from scratch. "In a few weeks" he "matured, more than in all the preceding twenty years." He learned of those who had not "bent their backs, lawyers, professors, and workers"; he learned the names of Gramsci and Salvemini, of Gobetti and the Rosselli brothers. The next step followed with an iron logic. When the Germans occupied the North in September 1943, Primo Levi took to the hills of his native Piedmont. Captured the following December with a band of Partisans as amateur as himself, he admitted to being a refugee "Italian citizen of Jewish race," thinking this safer than to acknowledge what he had actually been doing.[28] A catastrophic error—but one all too common among his coreligionists who had still not awakened to the full horror of what lay before them. Levi's next stop was in one of the recently established internment camps. By February 1944 he was on a train to Auschwitz.

Primo Levi's account of his ten-month stay in the place that has become the supreme symbol of Nazi frighfulness occupies a special niche in concentration-camp literature. Initially its distinction was less apparent: as discriminating a reader as Natalia Ginzburg rejected it for publication by Einaudi of Turin, obliging its author to take it to a less prominent house, where it appeared in 1947 under the title *Se questo è un uomo,* "if this be a man." Little by little over the next decade, as comparable books, more sensational and horror-laden, began to date, Levi's established itself as one of the rare classics in the genre.[29] By 1958 Einaudi reversed its earlier decision and from then on was to publish all Levi's subsequent writings.

What made his book distinctive? Above all, its tone—its tone of moderation, of equanimity, punctuated by an occasional note of quiet humor. By his own account, Levi had resolved to lift to a level of universality the unspeakable experiences he had been through—to compose "a serene study of certain aspects of the human soul." Rather than pouring out his indignation in a white-hot torrent, as so many others did, he fashioned his book in two stages: first he wrote his chapters "not in logical succession but in order of urgency"; only later, and with a calmer mind, did he fuse them together in accordance with a literary "plan."[30]

Much of what he wrote was familiar when it appeared; much has become still more familiar since. In particular, Levi took care to detail the special circumstances that had enabled him to survive. In common with others who lived to tell the tale, he freely recognized a series of fortunate accidents: his stay in Auschwitz proved short, less than a year; he was befriended by an Italian deportee, a civilian worker, who gave him extra food and clothing; his competence as a chemist eventually entitled him to sheltered work in the neighboring Buna factory, which was struggling in vain to produce synthetic rubber for the German war effort; most bizarrely of all, an illness that very nearly killed him saved his life. With the approach of the Red Army, the SS guards evacuated the bulk of the prisoners west—a gruesome winter trek, in which nearly all perished. Levi was one of several hundred too sick to tramp through the snow, who were left behind to await the Russians.

This final ten-day phase of survival, unguarded and abandoned to the bitter January cold, was the only one that Levi narrated in full grisly detail. And for a reason both moral and aesthetic: this was when the Nazis triumphed in defeat, when they broke the spirit even of those who had held out until then, when their former captives sank to less than men. As prisoner after prisoner froze or starved, the remaining human norms collapsed. "It is no longer man who, having lost all restraint, shares his bed with a corpse. Whoever waits for his neighbor to die in order to take his piece of bread is, albeit guiltless, further from the model of thinking man than the most . . . vicious sadist."[31]

Kameraden, ich bin der Letzte! Such had been the desperate cry of a rebellious prisoner at the moment of his hanging, in full view of his fellow-inmates, drawn up in ranks to the sound of a brass band. And such too was the final episode Levi chose to narrate before the great evacuation. The word "last" he never fully explained. But the implication seemed clear: the prisoner put to death had belonged to a secret ring of resisters and saboteurs that had linked camp to camp; presumably the others had been caught and slaughtered one by one; he, the victim, was the only man of courage left. Evidently the spectators thought so too: no "murmur . . . of assent" to his words rose from their ranks; they shuffled off in silence, overwhelmed by a sense of shame.[32]

In the carefully articulated structure of Levi's book this figured as the collective emotional climax. But it was an earlier episode, narrated in a handful of short, packed sentences, that gave the clue to Levi's personal universe of emotion and value, that unleashed his own cry of anguish. The moment was again one of unbearable tension: the periodic "selection" of the prisoners listed for death. Among those spared was an old Jew called Kuhn. That night, oblivious to the fate of his fellows, oblivious to the "abomination" which had just occurred, the wretch prayed aloud to his God, in the hearing of all, giving thanks for his deliverance. "If I were God," was Levi's grim comment, "I would spit out Kuhn's prayer upon the ground."[33]

Why the sudden breakthrough of passionate revulsion? Why did Levi turn on one of his coreligionists his strongest words of scorn? Perhaps the clue may be found in his repeated statement that he could "nourish" no hatred for the German people. He hated no people as such. If he and his fellow Italian Jews clung together, if they shared their sorrows and their tormented dreams of home, it was not through antipathy toward the others—it was because they were so helpless and so few. They did not form a great mass like the Jews from the East. They were not tough and resilient and adept at the arts of barter and theft like the Greek Jews of Salonica, "the most coherent national nucleus" in the whole camp. They were gentle, educated, and defenseless. "All lawyers, all with degrees," their numbers soon fell from more than a hundred to forty, since they were no good at manual labor, since it was easy to steal their food, since they were slapped from morning till night. "Two left hands," the Germans called them, "and even the Polish Jews despised them" because they couldn't "speak Yiddish."[34]

For such as these, the act of giving thanks for a special favor bestowed from on high smacked of a notion of Judaism that they had abandoned generations ago. The "ecumenical humanism" which had taken its place admitted of no limitations on a universal claim to sympathy. Thus, when on his return home Primo Levi was seized by an irresistible compulsion to reckon up what he had been through, it had nothing to do with paying off old scores; it meant to deepen one's understanding of an evil so vast and irreparable that it had permeated the lives of one and all. *Der Mann hat keine Ahnung,* the man has no glimpse of the truth, he wrote, relapsing into the German of the concentration camp, when, twenty-two years after the war's end, his former superior in the Buna chemical laboratory, who by an odd chance had become his business correspondent, suggested a friendly reunion. What shocked Levi was not so much the memory of the unfeeling way this man had treated him nearly a quarter-century before; it was the German's total incomprehension of the evil which he and his countrymen had either done or countenanced; it was the implicit request for "absolution"—coupled with the insufferable suggestion that Levi had transcended his own Judaism by following the Christian injunction to love one's enemies![35]

"Prisoners of Hope"

The same compulsion to plumb the depths of unparallcled human experience prompted Levi to pick up once more, after the lapse of a decade and a half, the thread of his wartime memories. In *La tregua,* "the truce," which he composed in the early 1960s, he told of the trials (and the absurdities) of the fully nine months after his liberation that it took him to reach home. The book read like a picaresque novel—a series of bizarre adventures and encounters with equally improbable characters drawn from a dozen nationalities. As though in anticipation of what his own future held in store, Levi had recalled in Auschwitz, Dante's haunting lines about Ulysses and his companions; in the spring and summer of 1944 he too found himself embarked on an odyssey, punctuated by a variety of mishaps, of detours, of leisurely sojourns in soporific meadowlands, that recalled his illustrious predecessor. In its narrative line his story wound its way through Poland and the Ukraine and Byelorussia, with no fixed direction, often simply going where the condition of rail tracks dictated, farther, in fact, from Turin than Auschwitz had been, until at last and inexplicably—like nearly everything else in the tale—the real journey home began, thirty-five days in all, through Rumania and Hungary, on via Czechoslovakia and Austria, and over the Brenner Pass to the Italy for which the narrator had sorrowed and ached with longing.

These wanderings constituted an odyssey in another and more profound sense. As Levi's first book had told of his descent into the inferno, so his second recorded his struggle up again to the land of the living, his effort to purge himself of the "poison of Auschwitz" that tormented his dreams, to wash his conscience and his memory "clean from the foulness that lay upon them . . . The months . . . of wandering on the margins of civilization . . . seemed . . . like a truce, a parenthesis of unlimited availability, a providential but unrepeatable gift of fate." In common with Carlo Levi, his namesake Primo had the happy sensibility of an amateur anthropologist: he knew the trick of turning boredom into education. "These virgin primeval horizons," he wrote of his departure from the lands in which he had so unwillingly tarried, "this vigorous people full of the love of life, had entered our hearts . . . and would remain there . . . glorious and living images of a unique season of our existence."[36]

Levi's undimmed curiosity served him well in the process of recovering his sense of himself as a human being. And the fellow human beings he encountered along his way—a mixed bag of hardy survivors—provided one after another the subjects he needed for a magnificent series of vignettes to document what he had learned and was still learning about mankind's infinite, its universal capacity to rebound from disaster. Some were drawn from his coreligionists. There was Cesare, the impudent youth from the Roman ghetto, shouting in triumph a new word he had learned—*meschuge*—to beat down the resistance of a reluctant customer in an improvised market. There were two girls from Minsk, dressed in black, at once demure and poised, returning home after thousands of miles of wandering throughout the Soviet Union, and incredulous that Levi could be a Jew, since he looked and spoke no differently from the other Italians traveling with him. In their country, they explained, "things were much clearer: a Jew was a Jew, and a Russian was a Russian; there were no two ways about it."[37]

What of the Russians themselves? It was toward them that Levi's steady, gravely ironic gaze was directed most intensely; it was from them that he learned the most about the common humanity he was striving to understand. He knew only a few words of their language; in Auschwitz his scientist's fluent knowledge of German had given him access to the mentality of his captors and a command of the lingua franca of their victims; on his journey home he was reduced to observation from the outside. But what he discovered rang true: he caught the maddening contrast between natural warmheartedness and official insensitivity that has baffled successive waves of subsequent visitors. The Russians who nursed him back to health, he observed, "lived together with friendly simplicity, like a large temporary family, without military formalism. . . . They were cheerful, sad and tired, and took pleasure in food and wine, like Ulysses' companions after the ships had been pulled ashore." It was in a similarly haphazard and undisciplined fashion that the demobilized men of the Red Army, whom he watched day after day along an endless road, trudged home— "often barefoot, . . . some singing lustily, others gray-faced and exhausted"—they scarcely seemed conquerors. Yet behind them (and him), he noted, lay "the inscrutable Soviet bureaucracy, an obscure and gigantic power, . . . suspicious, negligent, stupid, contradictory and . . . as blind as the forces of nature." This dread force had rounded up the collaborationist Ukrainian women whom Levi also saw coming home, crammed into "roofless cattle trucks," joyless and hopeless, humiliated and shamed. Levi "watched their passage, with compassion and sadness," as "a new testimony to . . . the pestilence which had prostrated" his continent.[38]

So he refrained from judgment on his Russian hosts. He took advantage, rather, of his enforced sojourn among them, to learn what they could teach, by action and gesture, of the colossal evil they had at once suffered, inflicted, and survived. On balance, their resilience and their vitality gave him greater reason for hope than for dismay. But long before his final release he was burning with impatience to leave: he had learned more than enough. And his deliverance came on an appropriate note of farce, again inexplicably, in the form of a *deus ex machina* emerging quite literally from a tiny car that seemed incapable of containing his huge bulk, no less a person than Marshal Semyòn Konstantinovich Timoshenko, hero of the Civil War and Stalin's friend, recalling to mind "the rough Kutuzov in *War and Peace,*" and delivering himself of the unbelievably glad tidings: "War over, everybody home."[39]

"The awesome privilege of our generation and of my people": so Primo Levi summed up what the vicissitudes of his wartime existence had taught him. Twelve years later he was prepared to add that his "baggage of dreadful memories" had become a "treasure."[40] The affirmative tone is startling. Yet Levi was not alone among Italian Jews of his generation to look back on their sufferings with a paradoxical sense of thanksgiving. "Tragic times have a perfume of their own," wrote a psychoanalyst of Levi's age from his new home in America, "and smiles of hope, and traces of charm."

"Why should a Jew let hope grow like roses in a garden? How can he have room for anything but the weed of despair?"[41] The rabbi of a small Piedmontese community had found the answer. "Many times," he told his son, "Jewish optimism is born of despair. Only for prisoners of hope is there a sure tomorrow." "Prisoners of hope"—the phrase resounded down the succeeding iron decades as a message of constant reassurance for that same son. The image of the "prisoner" the father had depicted was authentically Piedmontese: of a rock-climber, like Primo Levi in his youth, who cannot turn back, who has no alternative but to struggle on, grappling for a sure foothold, never permitting himself to forget his danger, yet confident of his own power to climb upward toward his goal.[42]

4

The Moment of Recollection: Turin

Piedmont and its capital, Turin, offered the classic example of a major city and Jewish community that attracted the aspiring and the talented from the smaller communities grouped about it. These latter had long cultivated a rich and varied life of their own. During the centuries before the House of Savoy became forthrightly philo-Semitic, the Piedmontese rulers had alternated rigor and benevolence toward their Jewish subjects in capricious fashion.[1] On balance, however, the lot of the Jews in the northwest had been slightly better than that of their coreligionists elsewhere; their ghetto experience, at the very least, had been briefer. Of mixed origin, with a large Ashkenazi element, they included a number of prominent families whose names—Foa, Momigliano, Segre—suggested a southern French or Spanish derivation. It was the sons of such as these who sought their intellectual fortunes in Turin. Yet recollections of the little world they had left behind lingered on, reinforced by frequent visits back to old home towns which afforded an inexhaustible source of nostalgia.

Of the protagonists of the present study, half were Torinesi. All originally bore the same surname: with two Levis we are already familiar; the third, Natalia—known to literature by her married name of Ginzburg—suffered persecution as they did and, like them, survived to write of what she had endured. But in her case the fear and horror she had been through figured only tangentially in her writing; at its center was a struggle to come to terms with the *ambiente* in which she had grown up.

A distinguished Torinese scholar, Arnaldo Momigliano, has commented on the scarcity of Italian Jewish memoirs.[2] To this, Piedmont ranks as an exception, with a respectable sprinkling of autobiographical writings. If Natalia Ginzburg's *Family Sayings* has established itself as the classic in the genre, four comparable works may set the stage and delineate the context from which it emerged.

The Testimony of Four Memoirists

Of Piedmontese memoirists, Primo Levi logically comes first. Not that his book of recollections is in the strict sense an autobiography: entitled *Il sistema periodico,* it consists of a series of episodes, named after the atoms in the periodic chart and following only a loose chronological order. The first chapter is called "Argon," a gas at once "rare," "noble," and "inert."[3] Such, the author implied, was the traditional life in the Jewish communities of Piedmont, a life he knew at second hand through family memories. This family stemmed from the province of Cuneo southwest of Turin; it was "rare," not in its intellectual interests but in its scientific and technological bent; Primo's grandfather and his father were both engineers.

In their matter-of-factness the chemist's Jewish forebears seemed charactericaliy Piedmontese. Alongside his passion for science, Primo Levi loved the savor of words and, more particularly enjoyed tracing the way in which his twin traditions had combined over the centuries into a curious blend. The language his family had spoken, he noted, was the dialect of the Christians surrounding them—"rough, sober, and laconic"—intermixed with terms taken over from the Hebrew—"sacred and solemn"—which had been given Piedmontese inflections and endings. The result frequently lent itself to laughter. But this comic aspect remained unwritten and unchronicled. It held out against the onslaught of modernity in the speech of the old people, the innumerable aunts and uncles, called such by the young, since "all or nearly all the elderly of the community," if one pursued the matter far enough, turned out to be related.

Hence, Primo Levi, although city-bred himself, found his own "roots" not so much "sturdy" as "deep, widespread, and fantastically intertwined."[4] His appreciation and affection for the far-flung kinship network that helped sustain his spirits we find echoed in the firsthand and richly detailed memoirs of the Hebrew scholar and Zionist activist Augusto Segre. Unlike Levi, Segre lived until his late teens in a traditional Jewish community, Casale Monferrato, where his father held the post of rabbi and which was infinitely more important than that of Levi's ancestors.

Casale, almost due east from Turin, in the late nineteenth century had functioned "for two generations" as the Jewish "intellectual center of northern Italy." At that time its community had numbered over seven hundred; by the time of Augusto Segre's boyhood in the 1920s its Jewish population had been reduced by two-thirds and its earlier eminence to a golden memory.[5] But it retained a high status among Italian Jewry. And to the rabbi's son the complex still clustered within the old ghetto—the tiny, exotic shops, the ancient houses of friends and relations, the musty temple—conveyed a sense of familiar warmth and emotional nourishment. The austere Ashkenazi rite his father celebrated stirred the boy to his inmost being. At the moment of blowing the ram's horn, the *shofar,* children and adults alike were gripped by a profound, scarcely articulate consciousness of their responsibility as Jews. As the sound of the horn, "at first light, uncertain, tremulous," increased in volume and intensity until it burst forth and "invaded" the whole temple, as it hung "suspended in the air" and then weakened to "a lament" that slowly died away, the young Segre felt a "shudder" run over his body, felt himself pierced "down, down, to the very depths of his soul."[6]

As the service progressed, even the most dignified, the most eminent figure in the temple was "always filled with a joyous emotion." Professor Ottolenghi functioned in a dual capacity, as president of the Jewish community and principal of Casale's *liceo,* or elite high school. In the ambiguities he experienced in meshing the two, he may stand for an ideal type of the assimilated Italian Jew of secular learning and high station still loyal to his religious heritage. As a Jew, the "president-principal" behaved with discretion and a due regard for tradition, although "Hebrew was not his strong point," and he would argue with the rabbi over how strictly one should adhere to every minor observance. As a secular scholar, he prided himself on his "encyclopedic culture," on the fact that he "knew a large part of *The Divine Comedy* by heart," on the elegance of his oratorical style, a style which never deserted him, so that even in private conversation he seemed to be lecturing to his class. Which capacity had the upper hand? To which of his two worlds was he the more profoundly attached? An anecdote from Segre's years as a student at the liceo—he was already Bar Mitzvah, and Ottolenghi was a family friend—may suggest the answer. On the occasion of the heir to the Italian throne's narrowly escaping assassination, the students were mobilized for a torchlight procession of thanksgiving. As Segre was marching with the others, he felt the torch suddenly "wrenched from his hand, while the unmistakable voice of the principal . . . was saying *sottovoce:* 'Go to the synagogue to make up the *minyan*'"—the indispensable complement of ten adult males.[7]

It would be wrong to conclude on a lighthearted note. Casale's Jewish community underwent the usual quarrels and anxieties of the tightly knit. Nor had traces of popular anti-Semitism vanished entirely. By the time of Segre's childhood its overt expression among adults had almost ceased; but it had left its traces among schoolboys—most frequently in stupid, cruel mockery about pigs' ears. One day the rabbi's son came home bruised and bloody: he had stood his ground against his persecutors. In answer to his father's solicitous questioning, the boy reminded him of his own precept that a Jew should "know how to defend himself." "Bravo," you did the right thing, the rabbi replied, as he folded his son in his arms.[8] The experience was the reverse of a father's cowardice which so distressed Sigmund Freud. A decade later Augusto Segre, like Primo Levi, was to enroll in the anti-Fascist Resistance.

An older writer, a Catholic by faith and of Jewish descent through his mother's side, may further remind us of the darker aspects of life in the small communities of Piedmont. For the legal scholar and historian Arturo Carlo Jemolo, Jewish memory survived in his own sense of marginality, of an independent and personal understanding of the paternal faith, within his country's religious majority—and in his mother's recollections. These dated back to the decade from the mid-1870s to the mid-1880s, when the migration to Turin had already begun but the bittersweet taste of ghetto life had not yet been obliterated. In the case of Jemolo's mother, the Jewish group in question was too small to be called a community at all. In Mondovì, to the south near Cuneo, the old ghetto consisted of no more than two dwellings; the few Jews still in residence lived socially isolated from their neighbors within the "vast circle" of a single extended family. No wonder that in such circumstances the chronicle of life looked "wan." No wonder that through the constant intermarriage of cousins, the Jews' bodies became "small" and "weak."[9] Doubtless it was for the best that so feeble an offshoot of Judaism should wither. To depart for Turin made sense for one and all.

Ivrea, to the north, resembled Mondovì in that its mid-nineteenth-century Jewish population numbered fewer than a hundred and that it too eventually ceased to function as a community. Its chronicler, Davide Jona, with characteristic modesty never tried to publish his memoirs: composed in English for the enlightenment of his American-born grandchildren, they remain unfinished and in typescript form, as he left them at his death in 1971. When he himself was a child, in the early 1900s, the Ivrea community had already fallen below the critical mass requisite for survival. With only five heads of families who could be counted on, "it was practically impossible, except on very special occasions," to muster a minyan. In consequence, young Davide's religious education suffered: his father soon gave up trying to teach him Hebrew, and his Bar Mitzvah was, by his own admission, perfunctory. Yet in these unpropitious circumstances, a residual Jewish consciousness lingered on: both the boy's parents "strongly" affirmed their heritage as Jews, "if not by religious convictions, at least by origin, and mostly by a deep, ingrained feeling of belonging to a special group."[10]

In their son this ancestral consciousness was reinforced by two extraordinary sets of experiences. The first was the arrival in 1906, when Davide Jona was a child of five, of "some bedraggled persons" who claimed to be Jewish refugees from the pogroms in Russia that year. The boy's father was initially skeptical: when he tested the strangers by asking them to read from a book in Hebrew, their pronunciation proved "completely unintelligible." The elder Jona helped them out, nonetheless, and in the mind of his son there was planted "a seed which was bound to germinate later on. . . . I spoke a different language, I grew up in a different milieu: but from that time I knew that a bond existed between me and those poor scared men, a bond that I was neither able nor willing to reject."[11]

The second extraordinary series of events occurred after Davide, as he inevitably did, went to Turin in the autumn of 1919 for his higher education. Here he came into contact with a group of talented young men of his own age, left-oriented and already acutely aware of the Fascist menace. One of them—Adriano Olivetti, a distant relative—he had known as a boy in Ivrea. Adriano's father, Camillo, ranked among the five older men on whom Ivrea's Jewish community depended. A decade earlier, with the financial help of the elder Jona, he had launched the typewriter works which were to bring renown and prosperity both to Ivrea and to the Olivetti family—but no corresponding revival to local Jewish life. A newer friend was the future Resistance leader Vittorio Foa, whose sister Davide Jona married. Both these age-mates, young

Olivetti and young Foa alike, approached the anti-Fascist struggle with optimism and enthusiasm. Not so Davide Jona: to him ideological awakening gave scant comfort; by the end of the 1920s he was succumbing to "frustration," to something approaching "despair." As a tonic for his despondency he "started to be interested in exploring" his "spiritual heredity."[12] Unlike most of his new acquaintances, whose Judaism remained muted, he was one of the rare young Jewish freethinkers who drew from their ancestral tradition the courage to face the trials of discrimination and exile that lay ahead.

The Torinesi to whom Jona felt attracted, yet among whom apparently he never felt he quite belonged, included, besides Foa and Carlo Levi, the future novelist Cesare Pavese, the future publisher Giulio Einaudi, the future political scientist Norberto Bobbio, and the Russian-born Leone Ginzburg, their acknowledged intellectual chief. These were the militant anti-Fascists of whom Primo Levi, a half-generation later, had heard "almost nothing." Yet he had studied, as they had, at Turin's renowned Liceo Massimo D'Azeglio, whose most influential teacher, Augusto Monti, had befriended them and inbued them with a concept of literature as moral commitment.[13]

Of those I have listed, half came from Jewish families. Was this mere coincidence? One of the non-Jews did not think so. Half a century later Norberto Bobbio was to write of an "elective affinity" which made him "jokingly considered in the circle of his friends an honorary Jew. . . . None of the Jewish families" he "frequented was truly Fascist. . . . Not . . . that all" his "anti-Fascist friends were Jewish, but all the Jews with whom" he was "on intimate terms were anti-Fascists." Why was this the case? Bobbio was inclined to ascribe it to the Jews' "critical spirit," their "liveliness of mind," an absence of provincialism which made them less likely than most bourgeois Italians to be "overborne by traditional prejudices"—in short, to a "freedom of judgment" summed up by the word "radicalism."[14]

The young Torinesi, Jewish and non-Jewish alike, who studied, wrote, and argued together, lived a life of intense and exalted friendships. In *The Watch* Carlo Levi evoked with nostalgia their nocturnal walks under the plane trees of Turin's "vast and deserted" avenues, the "peripatetic . . . exuberance" of adolescents who had "important things to say to one another, things high and sharp like the white mountains in the background." A decade later he paid tribute to the leading spirit among them, to Leone Ginzburg, Russian-born but a resident of Italy since early childhood, whose bilingual, wide-ranging culture and utter seriousness of purpose both intrigued and awed comrades such as Levi who were older than he. With his "thick hair, tough and very black, with penetrating eyes behind his glasses, with the bushy shade of his eyebrows," Ginzburg looked the part of the Russian-Jewish intellectual. When the author of *Christ Stopped at Eboli* heard of his friend's death in the winter of 1944—"at a time when one did not even allow oneself to weep" for the loss of those one held dear—he simply penciled a cross, "between one sentence and another," at the point he had reached in the manuscript of his book.[15] The symbol may have been Christian, but its underlying religious tone was characteristically ecumenical.

The initial (and shortest) of Carlo Levi's three periods of imprisonment came in March 1934, just over a year after

Hitler's advent, under dramatic circumstances which marked the first time an *official* communiqué of Mussolini's regime had resorted to anti-Semitic language. Two young members of the Torinese branch of *Giustizia e Libertà,* Sion Segre and Mario Levi (who was not related to either Carlo or Primo), had been stopped by the police at the Swiss frontier as they were smuggling into Italy anti-Fascist pamphlets that could incriminate virtually the whole circle of their friends. Mario Levi managed to escape back over the border by swimming through the icy waters of the River Tresa. Sion Segre remained among the fifteen eventually arrested. Of these no less than eleven were Jewish, as the press took pains to underline, including four Levis in addition to Carlo, four Segres, and of course Leone Ginzburg. Most were soon released; Ginzburg and Sion Segre alone received extended sentences.[16] A year later, however, the police descended again. This time the punishments were heavier and the effects more drastic: Vittorio Foa was condemned to fifteen years, and Carlo Levi to the enforced residence in the South that was to inspire his writing. The organized anti-Fascism of Torinese intellectuals neverfully recovered from the blow.

To the family of Professor Giuseppe Levi, who were not originally from Turin, the two successive waves of arrests brought wondrous changes. The first revealed to the professor that his sons—among them the Mario who had swum to freedom—agreed with him politically: another son, Gino, shared imprisonment with his father in 1934; the third, Alberto, the constant companion of Vittorio Foa, went to jail the following year. On this second occasion the family began to sense that, through their anti-Fascist beliefs and activities, they were moving up in the world, were gaining a paradoxical social standing among the city's elite. To the wife and mother of those arrested it seemed that it was now the thing to do to be in prison. She and her husband "felt flattered" that their sons were in the same boat as a young man from "a very good family" such as Giulio Einaudi.[17] Turin was doubtless the only major city in Italy where such a cause for congratulation either existed or could be accepted as such.

Natalia Ginzburg: The Painful Apprenticeship

From the sidelines the youngest of Professor Giuseppe Levi's five children watched these extraordinary doings with bemused excitement. Natalia had been born in 1916 in Palermo, where her father, a noted histologist, taught comparative anatomy. She was only three when he accepted a chair at the University of Turin. Hence she grew up as a Torinese, but without local family attachments. Her father came from Trieste, and so, more remotely, did her mother, a Milanese by birth. With one parent Jewish and the other a nominal Catholic, the children received no religious education. When she anxiously asked her brothers what the family was, they told her "nothing"—it was not simply "mixed"; it was plain "nothing." So too was it neither rich nor poor, but rather "relegated to a neutral zone, amorphous, indefinable, and without a name."[18]

This sense of amorphousness haunted Natalia's childhood. She looked back on her education as marked by "inattention, incoherence, absurdity, and an absolute absence of any . . . defined and precise ideology." Certainly it was both casual and lonely: through an exaggerated prudence about contagious diseases, her father decreed that she should have her elementary schooling at home. He and his sons might feel certain of their own ideological stance; but they did not let Natalia in on the secret. Baffled and oppressed by the "mystery" of adult life, she took refuge in a private realm of fantasy, a realm peopled by the characters that some day, she hoped, would figure in stories and novels. Meantime, as the last of five, she suffered from being one too many, from the gratuitousness of her mere existence: decades later she would write with restrained eloquence of a sense of "guilt," of "panic," of "silence." Even the great city in which she lived, and which so many of her slightly older contemporaries loved profoundly, she found "melancholy" and shrouded in mist. Melancholy "pursued" her "everywhere. It was always there, motionless, limitless, incomprehensible, inexplicable, like a sky way up high, black, brooding, and deserted." But it was not so much sadness in her childhood that she recalled: it was stark "fear," fear of the sudden storms which punctuated her family life, the "angry voices," the "noises of doors slammed and of objects hurled," above all, fear of her father, a tempestuous domestic tyrant, to whom she dared address not a single word.[19] As a young wife and mother she was to be caught up in a horror surpassing the worst of her childhood imaginings.

Out of such a mental universe of pain, part real, part fanciful, Natalia Levi devised, with little or no encouragement, her apprenticeship as a writer. Unlike her two namesakes, who as mature men anchored in other professions found themselves impelled to put into words the extraordinary experiences they had undergone, she knew all along what she wanted to become. So too had Alberto Moravia. But he had never served an apprenticeship; his first novel had revealed his mastery of his craft. In Natalia's case, as with Svevo and her exact contemporary Bassani, the process of learning was slow and punctuated by discouragement. Unwittingly and from a distance, it was Moravia who taught her to write. With precisely this in mind, she "read and reread *The Time of Indifference* several times." From Moravia she learned that it was possible to embark on the "desperate undertaking" of seeking out the truth, which in the Italy of Fascism hovered "veiled and remote, like a spectre beyond one's grasp."[20]

Yet in the mind of the young Natalia the truth revealed itself as excessively schematic and abstract. In her early stories she kept her characters at an emotional distance: they were cruelly drawn and teetered on the verge of caricature. Their creator took care "not to specify the place" where they lived, "to situate them," rather, "in indeterminacy." And this for a curious and idiosyncratic reason: to Natalia it seemed out of the question that a family background such as hers could produce a writer. Nor could so sober a city as Turin; it would have been quite different had her experience been of Moscow or Petersburg. Still more, the fact that she was Jewish banished her "far, far away from the world of poetry." She "knew of no writer who was at one and the same time Jewish, of a middle-class family, son of a professor, and raised in Piedmont." She did know about Kafka, "but he . . . had not grown up in Piedmont." The result was a "horror of autobiography" (this from someone who eventually was to produce a masterpiece in the genre!), as of "feminine . . . sentimentality"; she "wanted to write like a man."[21]

Marriage lifted her out of the realm of the unreal and the indeterminate. During the imprisonment of her brothers' friend Leone Ginzburg she kept up a secret correspondence with him. On his release in 1936 he went to work for the new and struggling publishing house that Giulio Einaudi had launched, where Natalia too eventually found a second home.

Two years later she and Leone were married—in the very year of the anti-Semitic laws. Devoted to one another, the young couple, as both Jews and anti-Fascists, were condemned to a life of improvisation. Natalia gave birth to two boys in quick succession; Leone was imprisoned from time to time as a security measure. Finally, in June 1940, on Italy's declaration of war, Leone was sent to enforced residence in a small town of the Abruzzi. Two months later Natalia and the children joined him. Here the four of them dwelt in an oasis of precarious hapiness: Natalia subsequently recalled it as "the best time" of her life, for, as she specified elsewhere, happiness might well include "desperation" itself.[22]

Her reaction to confinement in a southern village inevitably invites comparison with Carlo Levi's. The place in which she was forced to live was far to the north of his—larger, closer to a provincial center, less impoverished, and with a more visible bourgeoisie. She had her family with her; he had none. Conversely, he had a profession that give him intimate access to the local people; she had none. For Carlo Levi the experience of *confino* was something central to his future existence, an experience he treasured the rest of his life. For Natalia Ginzburg it was something episodic and encapsulated, bittersweet, like dwelling in a ghetto; unlike Carlo Levi, she never returned to a place whose memory was tarnished by a fearful outcome.

The difference emerges in the literary products of their forced sojourns. *Christ Stopped at Eboli* expressed its author's sympathetic curiosity about the closed, mysterious world of the people who were to become *his* peasants; it was suffused with an affection that Natalia Ginzburg might well have dismissed as "sentimental." She herself never gave a full account of her corresponding vicissitudes. What she did instead was to write the first of the series of short novels which gradually won her renown: *The Road to the City.* Where Carlo Levi was all warmth and compassion and literacy flourishes, Natalia Ginzburg imposed upon herself a dry factuality, the cool stance of an external observer, with an undercurrent of suppressed rage. She wished, she declared, that "every sentence should be like a whipping or a slap." Only one of her characters could be called *simpatico.* They were not true peasants, such as Carlo Levi had depicted, but peasants on the margin of the lower middle class, a status to which they aspired and which, at the end, her protagonist attained.[23]

To have written of them in any other way might have given her too much pain. The local people in fact had treated her with kindness, and she had learned to make friends of them. As a city-bred young woman, she had discovered a new world of rural life; she had been able to spend far more time with her husband than had been possible in Turin; with her little boys she had walked daily to a nearby meadow which offered a haven of tranquillity; in the early summer of 1943 she had given birth to a daughter. But a few weeks thereafter the fragile idyll of this parenthesis in her existence had come to an end. With the fall of Mussolini and the liberation of the anti-Fascists held captive, Leone felt compelled to resume his political activity, initially in Rome, then in Turin, and then once again in Rome. At first Natalia and the children remained in the place that had become almost a home. When, however, in September the Germans began to overrun the country, she too found herself in danger. Taking her children with her, after a perilous, nerve-wracking journey she joined her husband in Rome. It was now late autumn; they were together less than three weeks. On November 20 Leone was seized and hauled off to prison. In mid-winter Natalia learned that he had died—of beatings, of a heart attack, no one was quite sure. She was left a young widow of twenty-seven, with three small children on her hands.[24]

She never could bring herself to write in anything beyond fragments of her husband's end. And when she did so, it was in a tone of utter desolation. She spoke of the "icy February" in which she had heard "the horror of his solitary death," of an "irremediable . . . sorrow" that had "dashed to pieces" her whole life, of an unhappiness that was not merely a "tearful and anxious questioning," but an "absolute, inexorable, and mortal knowledge" of what grief could be.[25] At long intervals she would wrench out a phrase or two which gave a glimpse into the depth of her suffering. That was all. Her apprenticeship was over.

Natalia Ginzburg: The Arrival and the Departure of the Jews

Given the excessive "indeterminacy" of Natalia Ginzburg's early writing and her notion of the incompatability between literature and Judaism, it is perhaps not surprising that it took a long time for explicitly Jewish themes and characters to appear in her work. Yet it was as a Jew that she had endured the persecution which deprived her, as she put it, of peace of mind forever. And it was as a Jew that she had been sheltered in a Roman convent, sharing a room with a little old Viennese woman of similar origin, who helped take care of her youngest child, who served her tea, and who gave her and received from her "a sort of maternal protection."[26]

Curiously enough, living in Rome seemed to afford the distance she needed for appreciating which among the Jewish aspects of her childhood and adolescence in Turin had struck a responsive chord. For more than a decade she felt emotionally torn between the two cities. In 1945 she returned to Turin to work as an editor for Einaudi. Five years later, after her remarriage, she moved definitively to Rome. When she had first lived there she had suffered from a "profound nostalgia" for her northern home, even for its "interminable" winters and the melancholy she associated with them. In contrast, Rome, she wrote, "never sank totally into winter"; a "strange breath of leisure, of vacation, and of summer . . . could always surprise one in the midst of the cold." Turin held her early and deep memories, Rome those more recent and sharper, of the loneliness and anguish which made it "dear" to her.[27]

More curiously still: it was during her second marriage that Jewish themes came to the surface. Her first husband, Leone, had been more Jewish than she; but apparently he had not tried to steer her in this direction. Her second husband, Gabriele Baldini, professor of English and American literature, was a non-Jew six years her junior; but it was with him that she began to write of the people and places she knew best. An ebullient man, of a buoyant disposition, he helped to give her the confidence to write at last completely as herself.[28] The two decades of their marriage, until Baldini's premature death in 1969, were those in which she made her reckoning with her past and redeemed it from grotesqueness and fear.

When the Jews did enter, they came, as it were, on tiptoe. They came in the form of foreigners, at once exotic, annoying, and pitiful. They first appeared in the only extended novel Natalia Ginzburg was to write: *Tutti i nostri ieri,* "all our yesterdays," published in 1952. In composing it the author drew on her own wartime experience: the action moved from the ostensibly secure world of the urban bourgeoisie to a southern rural community caught up in an intricate set of personal dislocations. Among the latter there figured a handful of Jews—whom the police, for inscrutable reasons, had decided to scatter in small villages—poor people, including a family from Belgrade and "a Turk who was trembling with cold in a light-colored overcoat." "The Turk" kept bobbing up in the latter half of the novel, constantly complaining, anxiously commenting on the progress of the war, and consumed with terror that the Germans would find him out. And eventually they did: they loaded him onto a truck, and he was heard of no more.[29]

Natalia Ginzburg never gave the Turk a name or clarified his role in her novel—or only glancingly so, when the leading figure in the village, perhaps because in the course of his travels he had learned Turkish, declared that the stranger had become "his best friend." On another foreign Jew the author bestowed a fuller profile. Franz at least had a first name and was granted the honor of being shot in company with the same leading citizen for whom he had been only a vexation and a burden. Initially appearing in the guise of "the son of a German baron," always well dressed, preferably in white, and carrying tennis rackets, Franz soon admitted to having lied. He was neither German nor a baron: "he had grown up in Freiburg, where his father at one time sold raincoats. But his father and mother were Polish, and now they lived in Warsaw. And his mother was of Jewish origin and the Germans would kill her. He himself was listening to the radio all day long and weeping." Subsequently the full truth came out: Franz's father was Jewish also; he himself "was completely Jewish and it was well known what the Germans were doing to the Jews."

Franz and the Turk, although they "never made friends," shared a common obsessive fear and came to a similar grisly end.[30] If their creator pitied them, she scarcely showed it: she left them enigmatic and depicted from the outside. When, five years later, she drew her next Jewish character, a character more richly and recognizably Jewish, it was with enhanced sympathy and in greater detail. In the short novel *Sagittario* Dr. Chaim Wesser had a profession, a full name, and even a younger brother, "the only person . . . on earth" he "still loved." He was ensconced in an Italian family as brother-in-law of the young narrator. Once more, however, he was a foreigner, a Polish refugee from Nazi terror who had stayed on in Italy after the war's end, practicing medicine in a haphazard and skeptical fashion and frequently neglecting to ask payment for his services. Within the structure of the novel he remained peripheral to the main story of the swindling of the mother after the family's move to Milan from the small Piedmontese town of Dronero.

Moreover, Natalia Ginzburg left unanswered a perplexing set of questions about Chaim. What precisely was the attitude of the narrator toward him? Did she share her mother's sentiments of "benevolence mixed with scorn"? Possibly Chaim was too withdrawn to permit any simple judgement. Possibly a deterioration of personality had set in after his arrival in Milan. Clearly he had not adjusted to life in the big city: in Dronero he had been beloved, particularly by children, for his very eccentricities; in his new home he seemed cast adrift, going about with a "meek, bitter, and desolate smile" which revealed "teeth broken . . . by a fist in an anti-Semitic demonstration" back in Poland.[31] And similarly with his wife, the narrator's older sister: she too languished in Milan, pining away bit by bit until she died after giving birth to her first child. The novel ended with Chaim's sorrow left to the reader's imagination. But perhaps this was not so deep as one might suppose: the couple's affection for one another at the very least had lacked intensity, and Chaim had known too much of the world's evil. Perhaps better: both he and his wife had suspected all along that something of the sort would happen. Was the bond between them, in the end, a shared desolation?

By now it must be apparent that Natalia Ginzburg's Italians showed little or no hostility toward the foreign Jews whose fate (without the express intent of either party) through the circumstances of war became entangled with their own; the dominant attitude was one of pitying protectiveness. From time to time it could even be tender. The tone of tenderness finally emerged triumphant in the last of the series of short novels, *Voices in the Evening,* published in 1961. Once again, curiously, this little book, although without explicitly Jewish characters, came closer than any of its predecessors to tapping the wellsprings of its author's emotional world. As she herself explained, she wrote it toward the end of a second exile, more benign than the first, in London, where her husband's literary interests had taken her.

Overwhelmed by "a pungent nostalgia for Italy," she "all at once" found arising in her story, "unbidden," the scenes of her childhood, "the countryside of Piedmont and the streets of Turin." Gone were the inhibitions that had earlier held her back from writing about them; she had left behind "the old aversion and the old shame" they had inspired. Her characters had even acquired surnames, and it was with "joy" that she permitted herself to converse with them.[32]

One final barrier remained. While Turin was unmistakably Turin, although referred to simply as "the city," the small town, a short bus ride away, where most of the action took place, was left unspecified. It shared, however, certain crucial characteristics with Ivrea as transformed by the Olivetti family—and the Olivetti were closely connected with the author's own family. It lived by one industry alone; the founder of the firm, like Camillo Olivetti, had been a Socialist; his son and heir, in common with the younger Olivetti, Adriano, "knew a world of things" and "had many plans in his head." Still more, in the only Jewish note in the whole story, the patriarch accused the unkempt boy of looking like a rabbi. (Yet the same boy was later to become an enthusiast for "the Christian Left".)[33] And the novel progressed, and father and son both died, the family business receded into the background, and the doomed love of a younger son for the narrator herself moved to center stage.

"It was something very slight, very fragile, ready to break up at the first puff of wind." The young man proved unable to sustain it, and in the end he abandoned the childhood playmate with whom he had passed long afternoons in a rented room in Turin and to whom he had become engaged. "Why have we ruined everything?" was her lament—a phrase repeated three times in the course of the story. Perhaps it was because they had not been able to bring themselves to believe that happiness truly existed. "Happiness," the older brother had explained, "is like water; one realizes it only when it has run away."[34] Both men forfeited whatever happiness they had attained, and in the course of so doing inflicted irreparable grief on the women who had loved them.

By the time she wrote *Voices in the Evening* Natalia Ginzburg at last felt free to sound a new note, gentle, tender, diaphanous, a note of sad tranquillity. Though she had muted the desperate urgency of her earlier writing, the desolation of life was with her still. She had yet to venture, as her contemporaries were doing, into a world of trust and of hope. And she had yet to write without disguise of her childhood and youth. For this task—if task one may call the joyful transcription of "pure memory"—for the "only book" which, by her own account, she wrote "in a state of absolute freedom," she found precisely the tone she needed, a tone of delicate irony, veined with cordial affection.[35]

The autobiographical work *Family Sayings,* published in 1963, completed Natalia Ginzburg's progress from "indeterminacy" and cool detachment to an explicit recognition of her origins. Yet it was not an autobiography in the conventional meaning of the term. If it was, as the author readily confessed, the story of her family, it was a story with "gaps and omissions" which needed to "be read as though it were a novel." Its title suggested that the link connecting its episodes and personalities would be a "lexicon" of the expressions which still provided "the foundation of . . . family unity. . . . One word, one phrase" would be "enough, one of those ancient phrases, heard and repeated an infinite number of times in our childhood. . . . One of these would make us recognize one another, in the darkness of a cave or among millions of people."[36]

For author and reader alike the technique of letting individual family members define themselves by the expressions they added to the household jargon provided a welcome catharsis. It transmuted fear into comedy. How could one any longer tremble in dread before a father whose greatest feat, celebrated through constant reiteration, was once long ago in Spitzbergen to have "got inside the cranium of a whale"?

More particularly, how could his daughter regard him as infallible when the renowned professor of anatomy had not succeeded in locating the creature's "cerebro-spinal ganglia"? In Natalia Ginzburg's portrayal of her father there was both demystification and revenge for what she had suffered at his hands. Toward her mother she showed greater indulgence: though the maternal sayings might reverberate down the years as a succession of inanities, the figure who gave voice to them emerged as warmhearted, devoted to her husband and children, eternally fussing over every minor calamity, yet cheerful and courageous in a crisis—one might go so far as to say, a non-Jew who had ultimately become a mild version of the proverbial Jewish mother. In the final conversation their daughter recorded between her parents, they were still bickering—predictably about the whale—but there was no more shouting or slamming of doors; a tone of gentle mockery had prevailed.[37]

Husband and wife might seem temperamentally ill-matched; but on the fundamentals they agreed, on family and ideology, the very matters on which Natalia could recall only incoherence in her upbringing. Among these fundamentals Socialism took high rank: it held the couple together in their domestic fortress against the menace of Fascism outside. The senior statesman of Italian Socialism, Filippo Turati, was a family friend; it was in Giuseppe Levi's apartment that Turati hid for more than a week before his spectacular escape by motorboat from the Riviera to Corsica. As a child of ten, Natalia kept the secret; so too she held her tongue eight years later when, on the second occasion that historic events touched the Levi household, her father and brothers were jailed for militant anti-Fascism.

It was a Jew—Carlo Rosselli, the future founder of

Giustizia e Libertà—who had managed to smuggle Turati out of the country. And it was a half-Jew, Adriano Olivetti, who drove the car that took the old and ailing Socialist leader from Turin to the coast. Adriano had been introduced to the Levi family as a friend of Natalia's brother Gino (who was later to work as an engineer at the Olivetti factory in Ivrea); after overcoming his natural timidity, he succeeded in marrying her older sister. There was little about this "pale and fat" young man to suggest the future of visionary industrial leadership that lay ahead of him. "He was diffident and taciturn, and when he did speak, he spoke slowly with a very deep voice, and uttered a number of confused and obscure remarks, while he gazed into space with his little blue eyes, which were at once cold and dreamy." But events were to prove that beneath this awkwardness Adriano had both steel and kindness in his soul. Two decades later he appeared in Rome precisely at the moment he was most needed: when Leone Ginzburg had been arrested for the last time. Natalia recalled with infinite gratitude "the great relief" she "felt that morning on seeing . . . the well-known figure . . . familiar . . . from childhood, after . . . hours of solitude and fear." She would "always remember his back bending to gather up . . . the children's shoes, with gestures of humble goodness, patient and compassionate." And when they left the house "he was wearing the expression he had . . . when he came . . . to take Turati away, out of breath, frightened, yet happy," the expression "he had when he was escorting someone to safety."[38]

Adriano's mother had been Protestant, and he flattered himself that such crossbreeding endowed one with special merit. His father, Camillo, who also became a friend of the Levi family—their Socialist and anti-Fascist sympathies drew them together—had something of the Jewish patriarch about him. "Delicate and noble" of face, with a white beard, he mixed "the Bible, psychoanalysis, and the preaching of the prophets" in his conversation. "He had a small falsetto voice, rather sharp and childlike," from which a bizarre sound effect emerged when he and Professor Levi met. "Both of them wanted to talk at the same time, and they shouted at each other, one in his falsetto . . . , the other in tones of thunder."[39]

To recall what was comic in Jewish associations served to draw their sting and to postpone for the greater part of Natalia's memoir the tragedy that lay ahead. Even about Leone his widow managed to dredge up from her memory an appropiate jest. On first meeting him, her father had complained that he was "very ugly"—like "all Jews." Her mother had reminded the Professor that he too was Jewish; at which, nothing daunted, he had readily concurred in his own ugliness. *His* mother, the paternal grandmother, moved with sprightly querulousness through her granddaughter's pages. A sometime beauty from Pisa, raised in luxury, she clung tenaciously to her Judaism. Appalled by the irreverence of her son's family, she would go about lamenting—as her particular contribution to the household jargon—that they made "a bawdy house of everything." At first she had opposed the marriage of Natalia's parents, under the misapprehension that the bride came from a line of devout Catholics. "She was constantly afraid," her granddaughter recalled, "that one of us out of sheer spite would christen her. The reason for this was that on some occasion one of my brothers by way of a joke had made the gesture of baptising her. Every day she said her prayers in Hebrew, without understanding anything, since she did not know the language. She had an aversion for people who were not Jews, just as she had for cats. My mother was the only exception. She was the only non-Jewish person, all her life, for whom she had any affection. My mother for her part was fond of her and used to say that in her self-absorption she was as innocent and simple as an infant at the breast."[40]

The lightness of tone could not be maintained forever. Sooner or later the harshness of the world outside was bound to intrude on the comedy of *Family Sayings.* It came, predictably enough, in the form of Jewish refugees from abroad. As had happened to Davide Jona a generation earlier, Natalia Ginzburg awoke to the threat that hovered over her Jewish heritage through meeting fellow-Jews who had fled from Germany, some of whom had found work in her father's laboratory. By the time she began her rather desultory university studies her three best friends were all from Jewish families, young women who did their best to be kind to the new arrivals. "These people were stateless. It was possible that we too might soon be stateless, compelled to wander from one country to another, from one police headquarters to another, without any more work or roots or family or homes."[41]

Natalia Ginzburg had arrived back where she had started, back to the plight of the foreign Jews who had sought shelter in Italy. But with a crucial change: in *Family Sayings* she allowed her fellow feeling for them, the premonition which had gripped her that she was marked out for a similar fate, to penetrate the gently ironic surface of her prose. And from that prose the Jews departed as unceremoniously as they had arrived: after *Family Sayings,* recognizably Jewish characters ceased to figure in Natalia Ginzburg's stories.[42] In the end, the memories she had evoked proved powerless to give sustained comfort, to convert into a cosy refuge the childhood home which had originally filled her with a sense of amorphousness and dread. Her time of hope had been too brief; her experience of persecution and death had seared her too cruelly. She remained haunted by the ancestral theme of exile. Seven years after she published her memoir it struck her once more as she glimpsed her small American-born grandson, hand in hand with his father, crossing a Roman street. "His walk, his long and proud and delicate head, his dark and deep glance, all at once made me discern in him something Jewish that I had never seen before. He also looked to me like a little emigrant. . . . The world had revealed itself to him as changeable and unstable; there had perhaps arisen in him a precocious knowledge that things were threatening and fleeting. . . . Little Jew without a country."[43]

If there was much of exile, there was little of *senilità* in Natalia Ginzburg's writings; she was far too vibrant a spirit to succumb to that particular variety of malaise. To these she added a third theme—again a variant on something eternal—the theme of a family in which private life and public concerns were inextricably entangled. For centuries the Jewish family, debarred a role in the wider society, had performed a public function even more notable than that of its gentile counterpart; the Fascist renewal of oppression had revived this age-old function. In standing up to Fascism, Natalia Ginzburg's family had proved itself "rich in true heroism." Yet its members had performed their heroic deeds in the context of the "small daily dimensions" of life, "without harangues and flexing of the muscles." *Family Sayings,* in its quiet, ironic fashion, established a model and set an example: in the deceptively unassuming form of a "diary of personal doings," it demonstrated how father, brothers, brother-in-law, husband, and the author herself had little by little entered into "the troubled national life," had been tossed about by it, and had emerged from the ordeal with a "dignity" totally free from false "rhetoric"—the dignity of those who have had greatness thrust upon them.[44]

5

The Moment of Recollection: Ferrara

"Ferrara," wrote Jacob Burckhardt, "is the first really modern city in Europe." It was the Renaissance precursor of what eighteenth-century Germany called a *Residenzstadt,* where "large and well-built quarters sprang up at the bidding of the ruler."[1] Modern in the sense having been laid out according to a plan, it had nevertheless taken the time-honored precaution of surrounding itself with walls. And down to the Second World War these walls remained, now overgrown and planted with trees and serving as a vast, half-deserted circular park. For in the intervening centuries Ferrara had failed to expand much beyond them; dwarfed by its neighbor Bologna, it had languished in the memory of past glories.

The Incomparable Walled City

Ferrara's walls loomed large in the writings of its native son Giorgio Bassani. So did the flatland around it, the sluggish Po branching into its marshy delta, and the Adratic seaside resorts to which the wealthier citizens fled for their summer holidays. Bassani was as viscerally attached to Ferrara as Moravia was to Rome. Or perhaps a better comparison would be to Svevo's

Trieste: "with a technique reminiscent of Svevo," Bassani unified his "world of characters" and gave a firm "horizontal dimension" to his stories through the "poetry of the streets" he named.[2] Yet unlike his great predecessor, the writer who restored Ferrara to the literary map of Italy felt no reticence about identifying himself as a Jew. On the contrary, he alone among his contemporaries celebrated his Italian Jewish heritage as the underlying and pervasive theme of his work.

From one standpoint, the moment of recollection in Ferrara is a simpler subject than it counterpart in Turin. Here we have a smaller city, with its Jews more consciously and traditionally Jewish, and, as opposed to the large and self-confident intellectual elite of the Piedmontese capital, a single isolated figure. But these are surface simplicities—or aids to a clear focus. From another and more illuminating standpoint, it will very shortly be apparent that what Bassani discovered in Ferrara was more complex than anything the Torinesi had learned about themselves and their *ambiente.* Once again: he and he alone probed Italian Jewishness to the depths of ambiguity, to its hidden sources of sorrow and comfort, and to an obsession with death, not as dread of extinction, but, paradoxically enough, as a means of cultural preservation—or even of ethnic survival.

Ferrara, like Turin, provided a classic example in the history of Italian Jewry: in this case, of a Renaissance age of gold just preceding the catastrophe of the ghetto. Under a succession of dukes of the Este family, it became what a contemporary called "the most secure refuge in Italy. . . . By this he meant to express the sense of tranquillity that the walls of Ferrara offered to the Jews, and in particular . . . . the sense of relief that those walls gave to the Marranos who, within their shelter, could free themselves from tribulation. For decade after decade they assured . . . . the return to Judaism of hundreds of Marranos."[3]

Immediately following the Jews' expulsion from Spain in 1492, the ruler of Ferrara had extended them a welcome. In the early part of the next century his grandson did the same for refugees from Central Europe, who by 1532 had become sufficiently numerous to found their own synagogue for celebrating the Ashkenazi or "German" rite. Eight years later a similar invitation went out to the Jews of Milan, who were beginning to feel the pressure of Spanish rule, and the year following, to those expelled from the southern mainland. Just after the mid-century it was the Marranos' turn to be welcomed without conditions; soon Ferrara became their literary and liturgical headquarters for the entire peninsula. But by that time the papal bull on segregation was on the horizon. The Duke refused to follow its provisions; what is more, he gave an evasive answer to a demand from Rome that he drive out his newly acquired Marrano subjects.

Such resistance was beginning to weaken when in 1598 the House of Este relinquished Ferrara to papal rule. Already a decade and a half earlier its Duke had consented to despatch to Rome three prominent Marranos who, as lapsed Catholics, suffered death at the stake. With the new century and the new overlordship of the Pope, the lot of the Ferrarese Jews grew steadily worse. In 1624 the ghetto was established. There followed the usual melancholy tale of loss of population and loss of wealth, physical debilitation and cultural decay.[4]

Although the Jews of Ferrara never regained the intellectual eminence they had once enjoyed, they continued to rank among the dozen leading communities of Italy. At the time of the unification (and their own emancipation) in 1860 they still numbered more than a thousand. In the decades following they succeeded in entering (and at the top) a field of endeavor from which, more than any other, Jews had traditionally been barred: they were very nearly unique among their coreligionists in becoming great landowners. This achievement could be ascribed in large part to the special circumstance that in the late nineteenth century the Po delta figured as a major center of drainage and reclamation. For such operations a steady infusion of capital was required; and this the Jews could supply. As early as 1874 we hear of a loan to an entrepreneurial consortium by a banker called Vittorio Finzi—incidentally, almost the only authentic Ferrarese name which Bassani was to introduce into his stories. By the twentieth century Jewish landed proprietorship was an established feature of local society. The sons of the substantial holders, who frequently had become lawyers or physicians, after inheriting from their fathers would continue to live in the city as agrarian absentees—now professional men rather than entrepreneurs, with their estates serving simply as sources of income and social prestige.[5]

In the early 1920's upper bourgeois such as these naturally gravitated to Fascism. Ferrara soon leaped to the forefront of the new movement, largely owing to the efforts of the dynamic Italo Balbo, who had a glittering career of national leadership ahead of him. He and his city typified the mobilization of north-central Italian landowners against the forces of agrarian discontent that was to aid mightily both in bringing Fascism to power and in steering it in a conservative direction. A year and a half before Mussolini's March on Rome, Balbo and his henchmen had cowed the Ferrarese countryside—and won the gratitude of agrarian capital, Christian and Jewish alike. In March 1921, of seventeen landowners who were persuaded to contributed to the support of Balbo's activities, six were Jews.[6]

If, then, Ferrara's Jewish elite stood at the opposite pole from Turin's in their attitude toward Fascism, the treatment they received after 1938 differed little from that dealt their coreligionists in the northwest. Nothing that happened in Turin equaled the destruction by local zealots in 1941 of Ferrara's Scuola Tedesca, or synagogue of the Askhenazi rite. The disillusionment of the Ferrarese Jews was correspondingly intense. Their sense of betrayal poisoned the atmosphere in which the young Bassani was struggling to find a precarious standing-ground.

A final turn of events gave Ferrara a lugubrious celebrity. It was here that following Mussolini's fall and restoration to authority in the North, the "civil war" between his neo-Fascist followers and his enemies began. In mid-November 1943 those who had rallied to the Duce were holding in Verona the founding congress of their new party. Suddenly word arrived that the Ferrarese party secretary had been assassinated. With the cry of "All to Ferrara," the gathering adjourned in disorder: that night the avengers slew seventeen anti-Fascists; four of them were Jews.[7]

Although born in Bologna, Giorgio Bassani regarded himself as a native of Ferrara. He had in common with Natalia Ginzburg the date of his birth, 1916, the fact that he moved in early childhood to the city with which his memories were to be entwined, and the further experience that the moment of recollection was to occur not there but in Rome. Toward Ferrara, Bassani entertained feelings at least as mixed as those

Natalia Ginzburg nourished about Turin; but in his case the ambivalence ran deeper. Decades after his departure, Ferrara still gripped him—and he seemed unable to write a substantial story set in any other city.

Bassani's father was a surgeon and a member in good standing of the city's upper bourgeoisie. The boy grew up taking social acceptance for granted and accustomed to a situation in which the leading Jewish families lived comfortably in the double world of assimilation and respect for their religious distinction. As an adolescent, by his own account, he was not inclined toward "examinations of conscience"; he preferred to play tennis and to chase after a succession of pretty blondes. One has the impression of a young man in perpetual motion and well-nigh inseparable from his bicycle.

On such a youth the shock of "racial" exclusion at the age of twenty-two descended with inordinate cruelty. It tore him from his accustomed world, pitilessly revealing the pettiness and cowardice in people he had regarded as friends. Nor could he fall back, as Natalia Ginzburg could, on the moral support of a family united in anti-Fascism of long standing. With characteristic reticence, he never wrote much about the ideological temper of the home in which he was raised. But what he noted down about his father's "confusion" and "misery" after 1938 suggests that Dr. Bassani conformed to the familiar model of the apolitical solid citizen who had trusted Mussolini and utterly failed to comprehend what had befallen him; his angry son took half a decade to learn to pity the broken, prematurely aged man.[8] The son too had passed through the bitterness of renunciation: he had been obliged to break his engagement to a young Catholic. In the end he married a woman from one of Ferrara's Jewish landed families.

That was in early August 1943, just a few days after

Mussolini's fall and his own consequent liberation from prison. In the intervening years the onetime carefree young man, his eyes opened and his spirit hardened, had become a clandestine anti-Fascist whom the police had duly tracked down. He had also become a writer. His first love had been music—and this early enthusiasm was to leave its trace in the impeccable cadences of his prose. But by the time he began his university studies—daily taking the shuttle train to and from Bologna—he had settled on literature. His notion of what the choice meant was both committed and wide-ranging. He had learned far more from a renowned professor of art history than from any of the specialists in his own field; he had studied not only the Italian classics but those of France and Germany, England and the United States. Initially he had turned his hand to poetry; it was only gradually and with great effort that he made himself a master of the narrative form.

Like Primo Levi, Bassani managed to circumvent the anti-Semitic laws and to receive his doctorate in 1939. But when he found a job, it was as a teacher in the segregated Jewish school of his own city. From that point on, with his energies absorbed in the anti-Fascist struggle, he was condemned to a hand-to-mouth existence. He worked under an assumed name in Florence, where the political ally who enlivened his evenings was none other than Carlo Levi, and in Rome, where he heard the dreadful news of Leone Ginzburg's death. After the liberation of the capital he supported his family as best he might, in one odd position after another, ranging from service as a temporary bureaucrat to a return to teaching. More particularly, a stint as scriptwriter for the cinema helped to focus his talents, to convince him that whatever technical devices he might borrow from his familiarity with film, a writer had "at his disposition no means beyond words and marks of punctuation." Slowly, as his stories began to appear, he gained recognition, first among literary folk, then, in 1962, with his *Garden of the Finzi-Contini,* among the wider public. Four years earlier, as editor for the publishing house of Feltrinelli, he had done both publics an inestimable service by rescuing from neglect *The Leopard,* the posthumous masterpiece of Giuseppe Tomasi di Lampedusa. By the mid-1960s Bassani had become a celebrated writer. He had also assumed the presidency of the conservationist society Italia Nostra—a post which befitted his anguished concern for beauty, whether natural or man-made, and his affectionate respect for his country's heritage from the past.

By this time Bassani seemed to have left Ferrara far behind. But such was far from the case. After his departure at the height of the Second World War, he had constantly revisited his native city and had meditated long and earnestly on what the experience of growing up there had meant to him. The result was a series of six volumes of stories and novels published between 1956 and 1972, which the following year he collectively entitled *Il Romanzo di Ferrara.*

The high-sounding title should not lead the reader astray. *Il Romanzo di Ferrara,* as finally constituted, was no majestic roman-fleuve such as Marcel Proust or Georges Duhamel or Jules Romains or Roger Martin du Gard had composed. It aimed at no sweeping panorama of the life of Bassani's city. It was rather a series of narrative vignettes, varying in length from a few pages to a full-length novel and only loosely linked together. If certain of the characters reappeared from volume to volume, it was in no more than one that each occupied a prominent position; in the others they received a mere casual mention. The narrator himself did not step forward undisguised until the second of the series. And it was only toward the middle of his labors that Bassani decided to group his books under a single title. As he had early explained in one of his rare interviews, he entertained no "literary ambitions reminiscent of Balzac." It was no concern of his "to present a general framework" of his society. He preferred "to write something which resembled the lyricism and the narrative tension of . . . [Svevo's] *As a Man Grows Older* and, above all, of Hawthorne's *The Scarlet Letter,*" a novel which he could "not reread without each time feeling the most violent emotion."[9] The American reference may strike one as farfetched—until one recalls that the book in question had a century earlier plumbed the agony of ostracism.

For it was the memory of ostracism which endowed Bassani's writing with its characteristic variant of nostalgia. Ferrara was the city that had both cradled and repulsed him. Almost of necessity his recollection, enriched with appropriate fiction, took form as a succession of privileged moments. And these he caught, as a filmmaker might, at the far end of a "corridor" of time, which "each instant" seemed to grow "longer."[10] "With apparently naturalistic means," he transported the reader into an "atmosphere of enchantment." It seemed as though he needed only "to pronounce a person's . . . name in order to create . . . the silhouette of that character, scarcely outlined by his pen and already fully drawn"—and the same was true of places, which he "more evoked than described."[11]

By a further necessity he wrote about Jews; these were the people to whom he had been closest in his childhood and youth. He combined and transposed the men and women he had actually known who stood behind his characters, and gave them names which, although authentically Jewish, were drawn from other parts of Italy. According to one account, he took them from the tombstones of the Pisan community's cemetery. Whether true or ben trovato, the mortuary derivation hits the mark. Bassani wrote of his characters in the elegiac mode—and with a peculiarly haunting funereal version of the familiar conviction of *senilità*.

Giorgio Bassani: To the Paradise Garden

The first three of Bassani's volumes proceeded in logical succession from the short works that appeared in 1956 with the title *Five Stories of Ferrara,* through the tight, classically constructed novella *The Gold-rimmed Eyeglasses,* published two years later, to the full-length novel *The Garden of the Finzi-Contini.* The second and the third the author left scarcely changed when he finally fitted together the pieces of his *Romanzo*. The first he had tinkered with ever since he had begun work on it as far back as 1937. His earliest efforts, he recalled, had cost him "enormous toil." And even after the series was completed, he went back to his original five stories, retouching them and giving them the new title *Dentro le mura,* "within the walls." Although the changes were mostly small—a telling phrase or detail added, a reference inserted to a character who would appear in a subsequent volume—they had the cumulative effect of making the stories more "realistic" and more solidly anchored in Ferrarese society. At least one critic has found a dissonance between this new version and Bassani's underlying and poetic flow of memory.[12]

The author himself stressed, rather, the process by which his city had advanced story by story from a modest "background" to the role of foil to his protagonists, and from an entity "a bit mythical," or a "small. . . invented universe, set apart," to "something concrete" and believable.[13] Within this larger process, Bassani's treatment of Jewish themes had progressed in four stages: initially through depicting ambigous relations between Jews and non-Jews; then through setting up an alter ego; for whom he next substituted his own person; in the end through creating a self-contained all-Jewish preserve in which a single lofty, enigmatic figure epitomized the subtleties and the perplexities of Italian Judaism.

The question Bassani addressed (while keeping himself far removed from the account) in his first two stories was a riddle of irremediable misunderstanding. Both "Lida Mantovani" and "The Walk Before Supper" dealt with the love of a Jewish man of high station for an uneducated Catholic woman of humble birth. In both cases the love proved unable to close the gap of social class between the two—a chasm deeper perhaps than that of religious difference. In both cases the bonds uniting the couple were physical and inarticulate. "Lida Mantovani" merely sketched the problem: most of the story concerned the girl's life after her lover had abandoned her, pregnant and inconsolable. But the author left with her the searing memory of her summer of cohabitation with her David—in a bleak room in a working-class quarter while his parents were off on their Alpine holidays—and the gnawing queries: "What was he looking for? What did he want? Why? To these questions there was no answer, and never would be."[14] Bassani kept his reader suspended in doubt: throughout his stories and novels he would sound an obsessive recurring refrain, *Chissà? Chi lo sa?*—"Who knows?"

"The Walk Before Supper" gave such questions a wider dimension. Here passion produced a marriage of half a lifetime, and here Bassani created his first fully drawn Jewish character. Not surprisingly, in view of the author's own childhood observations at home, Elia Corcos was a physician —and destined to be Ferrara's greatest, the object of "affectionate, unshakable admiration."[15] As a young man, one evening just before suppertime, he had gone to the simple home of the nurse whose animal affection he had won, he had proposed marriage to her father, and he had been accepted into her peasant family. Why had he done so? Why, unlike David, had he not walked out on her? Here too Bassani gave no final answer. But he offered a sequence of richly detailed circumstantial evidence which elaborated the consequences of the choice, and in so doing cast an eccentrically slanted light on the relations between Jews and non-Jews in Ferrara.

In asking for the young nurse's hand, Dr. Corcos had acted on no sudden impulse. On the fateful evening, with pale and fevered lucidity, he had confronted in his mind the "two paths" opening before him: the "rough, difficult, uncertain" climb to the heights of professional glory to which his medical promise entitled him to aspire, or the "smooth, easy, comfortable" course of remaining in Ferrara in the "modest life of a provincial general practitioner." Faced with such a choice, he had reasoned, who would hesitate? But was that all? Far from it. Dr. Corcos had withdrawn behind the hint of a sardonic smile and had stayed up until dawn, walking the streets and resolving on "Science" (with a capital "s") as his "mission."

Most people concluded that he had sacrificed a brilliant career. And for whom? For the nonentity Gemma, whom he had married. Perhaps here too the truth was shadowy. If it was clear that from the dawn of the day following his engagement Elia had seemed scarcely to see people any more—or better, to look at them "from above, as if from outside of time"—it was also apparent that his wife and his wife alone "had ever succeeded in penetrating beyond the barrier" of courtly politeness with which he kept his acquaintance at a distance. Was there some deep understanding between the couple which outsiders found inexplicable? Certainly there had once been a slender emotional support for the two in the person of Elia's father, old Salomone Corcos, a retired grain-merchant who had begotten twelve children, who had ended up living with his favorite among them, and whose infinite kindness had filled the house with an "incense" of benevolence.[16]

Toward Gemma her father-in-law "had always been human, affable, full of consideration." Not so her husband's other Jewish relatives and friends. The very situation and architecture of the Corcos home betokened a curious double existence. Located near the city walls, it faced on one side toward the open country and had the look of a rustic dwelling; it was from this direction that members of Gemma's family would arrive for a visit. The other side faced on a quiet city street and gave the appearance of a dignified town house of Ferrara's characteristic reddish stucco; from here Elia's callers would enter undeterred by the professional brass nameplate which intimidated Gemma's, and themselves intimidating the poor woman. They held the doctor's marriage against him—also his freethinking and the fact that he had settled far from the old ghetto quarter. But they still considered him one of their own kind and felt that "his growing success ... bestowed on their common origin a lustre from which sooner or later they too would benefit."[17]

In this conviction Elia Corcos' friends and relatives were

not mistaken. If his two sons received no Jewish education, neither were they brought up as Catholics. Although their father had ceased paying for a temple pew, he had the boys circumcised, and when the younger one died at the age of five, he insisted on burial in the Jewish cemetery, "alongside grandfather Salomone, according to the most orthodox ritual." In short, Dr. Elia Corcos exemplified to perfection the residual ethnic consciousness of the assimilated and universally esteemed Italian Jew. It was fitting that Bassani should add to his portrait, in a typically parenthetical phrase, that in the autumn of 1943 his eighty-five-year-old protagonist was deported to Germany, taking his lifelong secret to an unmarked grave.[18]

"The Walk Before Supper" was one of the stories that its author revised the most, tightening it and focusing it more precisely on the central figure. The third story, "A Plaque on Via Mazzini," underwent less reworking. Once again the protagonist came from the Jewish upper bourgeoisie; once again the theme of misunderstanding predominated. But here the failure to comprehend was collective and total: nobody in Ferrara, presumably not even among its Jews, could fathom why Geo Josz, the young scion of a wealthy family, had behaved so oddly following his return from Buchenwald.

He had arrived at precisely the right (or wrong?) moment in August 1945 when the survivors of the Jewish community, with premature haste, were having affixed to the facade of their temple a plaque commemorating the 183—out of a former population of about 400—who had perished in the gas chambers. Geo had found his own name among those listed as dead; it was evident that he alone had returned from beyond the Alps, albeit unrecognizable, "swollen with water, like a drowned man." For his part, he had straightway declared that "the plaque would have to be done over again"—or perhaps removed entirely.[19]

That was only the beginning of his bizarre actions. These occured in two phases. At first Geo had insisted that everything should be just as before. He had slimmed down; he had dressed impeccably; he had fought tenaciously, and in the end with success, to evict the former partisans who had occupied his family's spacious house; he had refused to talk about his concentration-camp sufferings. All this perhaps could be ascribed to a "secret dynamic relationship" between Geo and his native city: along with the collectivity of Ferrara, he was merely returning to "normal." What was harder to explain was his attitude toward two uncles who had also survived the years of persecution: he distrusted the one with an anti-Fascist record; the other, Geremia Tabet, who had ranked as *the* ultra-Fascist among the city's Jews, he had greeted with "a shrill cry, ridiculously, hysterically passionate, almost savage . . . , a kind of choked howl." Whereupon uncle and nephew had settled into an "instinctive . . . understanding," a tacit "pact" to forget the past.[20]

The following May all was transformed overnight. No one could ever adequately explain what had happened. On a street-corner at the edge of the old ghetto Geo had fallen into conversation with a decrepit nobleman, a sometime "paid informer of the secret police." More than one version circulated of the words that had passed between them: very likely the younger man had been subjected to too insistent a questioning. It was undeniable, however, since so many people had heard, that their talk had ended with two resounding slaps on the nobleman's cheeks. It was also beyond dispute that from that evening onward Geo's conduct had changed utterly. He now dressed invariably in his tattered concentration-camp attire; he discoursed with insupportable loquacity about what he had been through; people who earlier had welcomed him with sympathy now found him a public embarrassment and fled his company. After lasting more than two years, this second phase came to an end as quickly and as inexplicably as it had begun. One day in the summer of 1948, with Ferrara's return to something resembling the status quo ante completed, Geo Josz simply vanished without a trace.

Once more, what had happened? This time Bassani gave his reader a clue. There was "nothing enigmatic" about the crucial episode, he explained, nothing that an understanding heart could not unravel. The incident, he recalled, had occurred at twilight—at the hour when "things and people . . . show themselves for what they truly are." All at once, "as if . . . struck by a thunderbolt," Geo Josz had become aware of the sort of person with whom he was speaking.[21] And at the same instant his illusion of "normalization" had come crashing to the ground. Postwar Ferrara, he now saw, had no place for the likes of him. For a year or two he might try to teach it a lesson. And then he must depart.

The first three of Bassani's five Ferrarese stories were straight third-person narratives. Their author, by his own account, was shy about introducing his individual experience into the action. He had biting words for his former political ally "Don" Carlo Levi, whom he once described as never tiring of "looking at himself in the mirror" in the guise of an "exemplary figure." For his part, Bassani regarded his own person as something distinct from his best writing and worth "much less." True to this principle, he managed for a decade and a half "to keep himself concealed"—though with "all too fraternal" an attitude toward his characters—"behind the defenses, somewhere between pathetic and ironic, of syntax and of rhetoric."[22] By the time he reached his fourth story, "The Last Years of Clelia Trotti," these defenses had begun to crumble. As a transitional device, Bassani took refuge in the construction of an alter ego, whom he named Bruno Lattes.

To what extent should we regard Bruno as a stand-in for the author? That question of course forms part of the larger and more general one—applicable to all those who write quasi-autobiographical fiction in the first person—of the closeness or remoteness of fit between narrator and live human being, a question which arose when Bassani at length began to speak in his own voice. For the moment, it may suffice to observe that there was much in Bruno Lattes that recalled the author. Naturally he was Jewish; he was well versed in literature; he was an excellent tennis player; he was infatuated with a gorgeous blonde; his father languished in desolate disillusionment after the passage of the anti-Semitic laws; he himself taught at Ferrara's Jewish school. Yet in crucial respects his personality and course of life diverged from Bassani's own. His mother was born a Catholic, and he himself did not stick it out in Italy through the years of torment, sharing the fate of his parents, whose names were inscribed on the temple's commemorative plaque, but instead escaped to America, where he became a lecturer in Italian. As though to underline the difference, his creator subsequently took pains to introduce him into *The Garden of the Finzi-Contini* as a character separate from and even acquainted with the narrator. Then, slyly confusing the reader still further, Bassani had Bruno make a final appearance, in the last volume of the series, in three episodes, widely separated in time, which sounded like chapters from the author's own biography.

All in all, Bruno Lattes figured as less appealing, more mediocre and practical-minded, than Bassani (or the narrator). His function was perhaps to tread an alternative path, to embody what the author might on occasion have liked to be or to have done. Most notably, he gave voice to hidden, guilty feelings about being Jewish, the torment or even the hatred of that heritage. Listen to Bruno reflecting on his widely ramifying family: "What was there in common . . . between him" and them? Not only physically did he look very different but "even when it came to character, there was no resemblance . . . , thank God, not the slightest. Nothing flighty, excitable, morbid in him, nothing so typically Jewish. His character . . . was much closer to the strong, straightforward nature of his many Catholic friends." Or with even greater bitterness—this time Bruno dwelling with fascinated gaze on a blond, "Aryan" pair of young lovers: "More than beautiful, they seemed marvelous, unattainable . . . Their blood was better than his, their soul was better than his! . . . Oh, to be with them, one of them, in spite of everything!"[23]

It was logical, then, that Bassani should assign to Bruno episodes that rankled as particularly painful or even tinged with shame. One of them, quite predictably, concerned a non-Jewish blonde whose memory tormented his days and nights, who had shared his bed and had been his partner in tennis, and who had dropped him without explanation a year earlier—although one might suppose that the anti-Semitic laws had something to do with it. Now it was late August of 1939; the war was only a few days away. In this fevered atmosphere, Bruno was seized with an irresistible compulsion to see his former friend once more, to persuade her "to make love one last time." The idea was utter madness, he knew: "If the two of them were caught, she would end up at Police Headquarters like a common streetwalker, and he would be sent into forced residence." His "quick dash" to the Adriatic resort where his beloved was luxuriating was doomed to failure from the start. All that he got for his mighty effort was a family lunch, a swim—*and* a look at the swastika with which the girl's miniscule "demon" of a brother had adorned his bicycle.[24]

If to recall such a humiliation could make Bruno (or the author?) burn with rage and shame, its sequel—in time, not in order of writing—figured more perplexingly as a disappointment, a might-have-been. (We are back to the fourth of the *Five Stories.)* Here the reader met Bruno for the first time, a Bruno returned from America in the autumn of 1946 and witnessing the pompous civic reburial of Clelia Trotti. The woman so honored had been a forcibly retired schoolteacher and Socialist militant, who "had never submitted," who "had always kept her own spirit pure," and who had paid for it with year after year of poverty and lonely surveillance and, after the outbreak of the war, with death in prison. A quarter-century earlier the party leader who had been her lover had deserted her; so too, in a more remote and asexual sense, had Bruno. As he watched the ceremony proceed, he recalled how in late 1939, two or three months after his seaside fiasco, he had sought Clelia out and won her friendship. What had he wanted? Solace for his wounded male pride? A new and unfamiliar fellowship in his isolation as a Jew? What Clelia had wanted was far clearer: with gentle, almost flirtatious, insistence she had traced out for him a role of leadership in a revived, reinvigorated, youthful form of Socialism. And he had let her down: he had fled overseas. Perhaps it could never have been otherwise: night after night they had talked past each other. In their final conversation on the city walls he had scarcely heard what she was saying: he had been utterly absorbed in watching the aforementioned blond couple.[25] Once more we hear the note of irremediable misunderstanding.

But now, with Bassani on the verge of speaking in his own voice, the failure to follow another's thoughts strikes us with a crucial difference. This time we discover a second major personality in addition to a single enigmatic Jew: a non-Jew who shares the stage with him, and whose misfortune, whose *disgrazia,* is in counterpoint to his own. The rival protagonist is likewise an outcast. And the action follows the groping efforts of the two to sustain one another in a part-shared, part-alien experience of ostracism.

When Bassani advanced to the third of his narrative modes —when he finally began to use the pronoun "I"—the tacit sympathy between a forlorn young Jew and an individual expelled from "polite" society for quite other reasons became more explicit, and misunderstanding yielded to a new sense of human solidarity.[26] In the first of the short novels, *The Gold-rimmed Eyeglasses,* the protagonist or foil to the narrator-figure was not an outcast from the start, as Clelia Trotti had been. When the story opened, Dr. Athos Fadigati ranked as a successful and respected physician (although of course not remotely the equal of Elia Corcos). The discerning among the Ferraresi had surmised that he was a homosexual; but so long as he was discreet about it, they limited their recognition of the fact to an occasional mild and worldly witticism. Everything changed, however, when Fadigati—inexplicably, self-destructively—chose to flaunt his special friendship with a heartless young companion at an Adriatic resort where he could not fail to encounter a number of his prominent patients. *La disgrazia* descended on him with the iron inevitability of classic tragedy: loss of reputation, loss of clientele, and, in the end, suicide.

The decisive turning point by the sea occurred precisely in the summer when the anti-Semitic press campaign began. And with it, the young narrator, vacationing with his parents, who up to then had known Fadigati only slightly, began to sense that he and the older man had something in common. After both had returned to the city, their mutual need became more urgent. The narrator was overwhelmed by an "atrocious feeling of exclusion." He found gauche and unavailing the efforts of a comrade (the nephew of Clelia Trotti's old Socialist lover!) to remind him that in Ferrara at least it was impossible to draw a "sharp division between the Jewish 'element' and the so-called 'Aryan' element"; that "the 'Israelites' belonged, all or nearly all of them, to the most distinguished middle class of the city"; that "in a sense, they formed its muscle, its spinal column." Unconvinced, the narrator felt "born within" him, "with unspeakable revulsion, the ancient, atavistic hatred of the Jew toward everything that was Christian, Catholic, *goyish*. . . . *Goy, Goyim:* how shameful, what humiliation, what repugnance" welled up in him at expressing himself "in this way! . . . like any Jew from Eastern Europe who had never left the ghetto."[27]

So he ruminated in his desolation. It was only natural, then, that when Geremia Tabet (the ultra-Fascist uncle of Geo Josz) returned from Rome with an assurance from on high that "in Italy . . . no racial legislation" would "ever be passed," the narrator (quite correctly) refused to believe it. Nor could he stomach his father's joy at the glad tidings. It "was that of a child expelled from the classroom, who, from the empty corridor where he had been exiled to expiate a misdeed he hadn't committed, suddenly, contrary to all expectation, saw himself welcomed back in the room, among his beloved schoolmates: not only forgiven, but recognized as innocent and completely rehabilitated." At this point the young man's eyes happened to fall on an item in the local newspaper: a brief account of a drowning in the Po. Calmly he announced to his family, in one of the swift, terse endings that became Bassani's hallmark, "Doctor Fadigati is dead."[28]

The third volume of Bassani's series, *The Garden of the Finzi-Contini,* was the longest and by far the most popular. Its appeal lay chiefly in the love story running through it—the story of the unrequited longing of the narrator for the daughter of the family, Micòl: Jewish and blonde, attributes for once united in a single person, and equipped with appropriate literary interests. This aspect of the novel, puzzling or touching as we may find it, is not our concern. For the present study the predominant interest of *The Garden of the Finzi-Contini* is its portrayal of Italian Judaism. Not only did it go beyond its predecessors in promoting the narrator from a largely passive spectator to a full participant; it also dealt with the relations of Jews to each other rather than with outsiders. Nowhere else did Bassani introduce so many Hebrew words, such specific ethnic detail. Indeed, his whole cast of characters was Jewish—all, that is, except for the chemist from Milan, Giampiero Malnate, the friend of Micòl's brother, Alberto, and possibly her lover, whose positive, optimistic personality contrasted with that of the others in a fashion which Bruno Lattes might well have approved. (But Malnate was Communist, not Catholic; and the author deftly cut the ground from under his self-assurance by making his last action one of ideological betrayal: enrollment in the Italian expeditionary corps that accompanied the German invasion of the Soviet Union.)

The time once again was the autumn of 1938, the dread autumn of the anti-Semitic laws. The center of the action was a tennis court set in a vast garden, the private court of the Finzi-Contini family, on which Ferrara's young Jews from "good" families had been invited to play, after their expulsion from the local club. If the setting might appear tame, the circumstances of the invitation were far from banal. For the Finzi-Contini, with their palatial residence close to the city walls, with the thousands of acres from which they drew their income, were both excessively rich and obsessed with their own privacy. Half a decade had passed since they had last been seen in public, since they had undertaken to restore for their personal use a small synagogue of the "Spanish" rite, abandoned three centuries earlier. Before this withdrawal, it was true, the narrator as a boy had enjoyed a nodding acquaintance with them—but only through the accidental circumstance that his family and theirs sat in pews "one behind the other" in the "Italian" rather than the "German" synagogue, which shared the same temple building.[29]

The host thus depicted as providing a refuge for his young coreligionists ranks as the greatest of Bassani's Jewish characters—more fully drawn, more baffling than Elia Corcos or Geo Josz or even his own daughter, Micòl. In devising the personality of Professor Ermanno Finzi-Contini, the author pulled together a wider scattering of memories and historical fragments, a deeper set of apparent contradictions, than ever before or after. It was as though he wanted for once to offer a glimpse into the spiritual universe of Italian Judaism *beyond* assimilation, to devise a human being at ease or, better, unashamedly proud within perplexities that left others at a loss. But if this was Bassani's intention, he took care not to dot the i's or to cross the t's in his account. He exposed his clues without commentary and at widely spaced intervals throughout his book. He left it to his reader to fit the pieces together, to solve an apparent enigma. Or perhaps he trusted that reader to decide for himself to what extent the Professor could serve as the epitome of a "good" Jew in a twentieth-century Italian context.

The basic facts were simple enough: in 1938 Ermanno Finzi-Contini was seventy-three, with two grown children and a wife twenty-five years younger; he was a man of studious habits with a splendid library (though how and in what field he had acquired the title of professor remained unclear); his grandfather had risen from humble origins to the status of great landowner at the time of the emancipation of Ferrara's Jews; his father had moved into and "modernized" in Gothic style a Renaissance princely abode; his mother, strikingly handsome and of haughty bearing, had come from the baronial family of Artom. With details such as these—more particularly the Artom connection, which situated the Professor within Italy's most distinguished Jewish lineage—[30] Bassani displayed an unerring feel for the gradations of economic, social, and educational level against the shared "bourgeois" background of Italian Jewry.

Still more adroitly, the author allowed the narrator's father to convey much of the information: a reporting tinged with hostility, which the son, on closer acquaintance with the subject, could little by little rectify. To the older man, physician, "sports enthusiast," and freethinker, who thought of himself as a "modern Jew," the Finzi-Contini appeared snobbish nouveaux riches, bigoted but at the same time not "even. . . like *judím*"; their self-imposed isolation betokened nothing more mysterious than misplaced pride, a covert anti-Semitism.[31]

How could one reconcile this view with the Professor Ermanno whom the narrator came to know after the invitation to the tennis court and, still more, when, on his exclusion from the municipal library, he began to work day after day in the magnificent collection adjoining the Professor's study? How could one square the cordiality of his welcome as a fellow-scholar, his host's exquisite courtesy and thoughtfulness, conveyed in a "pleasant, musical voice," with the unappealing object of his father's verbal barbs? The answer was necessarily veiled. It gradually (but never completely) unfolded as a "secret," intensely private vision of Judaism in the contemporary world, a secret which the narrator was extended the honor of sharing. For the Professor had designs on his guest: like Clelia Trotti with Bruno Lattes, he had traced a "plan" for the young man's future, a plan obliquely conveyed by the barely voiced suggestion that he might become "one of the shining lights of Italian Jewry."[32]

The key to the matter, one may guess, "was the one thing . . . in his study," cluttered with the miscellaneous accumulation of a lifetime, at which Professor Ermanno "never smiled": "an enormous life-size portrait" of his mother. The blonde baroness had been half-German; in her pride she had nourished a "*fundamental anti-Semitism.*" (The italics are Bassani's.) In an evident reaction against such sentiments, her son had made a totally different marriage. As a middle-aged bachelor, long after his mother's death, he had chosen for his bride a young woman, or rather "girl," with a "fanatical . . . glow" in her eyes, from the "*very* good" but "ultra-observant" and Sephardic Herrera family of Venice. The Finzi-Contini shared their pew in the temple with two Herrera brothers, who never married, who frequently came to visit, and whose passionate, demonstrative devotion to traditional Judaism surpassed even that of their sister. It was to please these three, so the "official" story ran, that Professor Ermanno had restored the little synagogue in which they could celebrate the rite familiar to them from childhood. But the narrator knew better. He "knew perfectly well" that the real reason was the Professor's desire to shut himself off at a time when one and all had been urged from on high to join the Fascist party, and he had refused. And, as though to confirm this interpretation, when five years later the party and the regime swung over to anti-Semitism, the Finzi-Contini family in full force solemnly reentered the Italian synagogue for Rosh Hashanah. As Micòl put it, "We're all in the same boat now."[33]

On one point, however, the narrator's father turned out on balance to be right. Although Professor Ermanno may not have "actually liked the racial laws," as his critic claimed, "basically he didn't seem to mind very much. . . . On the contrary," the narrator noted on his first invitation to the Finzi-Contini dinner table, the family greeted the new situation with little surprise and with "elegantly sarcastic . . . comments" delivered in a tone of gaiety and even satisfaction. Perhaps this well-bred hilarity betrayed a sense that the resegregation which so distressed other Jews admirably fitted the Professor's "secret plan." Perhaps, to quote the narrator's father once again, it was not too farfetched to suppose that Ermanno might on occasion dream of subdividing his vast garden "into a kind of *kibbutz,*" under his "own exalted patronage." Certainly the benevolent glow of affection that greeted the young man when, escaping from his own family's gloomy Passover celebration he joined the Finzi-Contini at their festive table, suggested a novel and yet age-old "solidarity" into which he was being initiated.[34]

So whether or not the Professor deep in his heart nourished

a nostalgia for the ghetto, he stood ready to provide the sort of cosy refuge that sentimentalizing memory could make of it. Of course its inner circle would be limited to a few, to the few who at least dimly understood and measured up to the Finzi-Contini notion of Jewish distinction. For them the garden unfolded its mysteries as an oasis of serenity in a world of desperation. As for the narrator, the mere recollection spelt "paradise."[35]

Was Ermanno too a "prisoner of hope"? Yes, in the sense that he, as Bassani had observed in an earlier story, felt the need of a "little margin of illusion" in order "to go on living."[36] For his daughter, Micòl, the "margin" lay rather in memory. And so it was also for the narrator, who had shared her "vice" of looking to the past even while he had loved her in vain. (Possibly it was for that very reason that her father's "plan" left him perplexed.) In this regard the two young people proved less prone to illusion than the elderly scholar, for all the weary skepticism of his perpetual courtly smile. "The dear, the sweet . . . past"—a past to be touched only with gentle, pious hands—was to provide a surer refuge for flickering hope than a nebulous design to rekindle, through fastidious disengagement, "the shining lights of Italian Jewry."[37]

Giorgio Bassani: The Splendor of Death

With Micòl's cult of memory, Bassani stood on the threshold of a celebration of death. But as though he was not yet ready to enter that dark domain, he confined his remarks to hints and foreshadowings. He cast his prologue to *The Garden of the Finzi-Contini* in the form of a visit to Etruscan tombs north of Rome, thereby allowing himself to be reminded that the family had been carted off to Germany to die. Few further details were vouchsafed the reader: Bassani ended his novel still more abruptly than was his custom; he disdained even to confirm or refute the narrator's suspicions about the relations between Micòl and the non-Jewish chemist Malnate. He seemed as yet incapable of destroying the "atmosphere of enchantment" he had evoked, unwilling to bring himself to shatter it with an eruption of evil.

In *The Gold-rimmed Eyeglasses* the narrator had been only lightly touched by the evil that befell Dr. Fadigati. In *The Garden of the Finzi-Contini* it came closer—with Malnate's secretiveness and presumed treachery, with the lingering, agonized death of Alberto a year before the deportation of his parents and sister. If Bassani had merely wanted to have his say about prewar Jewish life in Ferrara, he might well have stopped here. But the riddle of evil beckoned—and with it the awesomeness of death, as ultimate disaster and sovereign remedy alike. More concretely and historically, two further self-imposed assignments lay ahead: to fill in the hiatus of adolescence left in suspension when, at the close of the first part of the Finzi-Continis' story, the childhood "flirtation" between the narrator and Micòl had broken off; to give a fuller account than Geo Josz's contradictory behavior could furnish, of the situation of Ferrara's Jews after their persecution came to an end, and in so doing to depict a profoundly troubling figure as a counter-player to Professor Ermano himself.

With *Behind the Door* (1964) and *The Heron* (1968) Bassani returned to the short novel form. The first was the least Jewish of his stories and the only one in which the narrator held the center of the stage. The protagonist and his schoolmates were still in their mid-teens; the anti-Semitic laws were still nearly a decade away. What loomed as of overriding importance was not whether one was Jewish or Catholic, but how one formed and kept friendships and approached the perils of sexuality. In this respect *Behind the Door* recalled the self-torment of Moravia's adolescents or, rather more, the murky sadistic entanglements of Robert Musil's *Young Törless.* In what the narrator described as one of the blackest periods of his life, when he received "a secret wound" which he never "managed to heal," it was not as a Jew that he suffered; it was as a boy uncertain of his position among his peers.[38]

Yet an eternal Jewish theme lay just beneath the surface: the sense of ostracism, of having been excluded, which the narrator was subsequently to feel so cruelly and which was a variant on the theme of exile. The sting of betrayal inevitably accompanied it. With a characteristic rejection of the explicit, Bassani left the identity of the outcast long in doubt. It certainly was not the self-assured and quietly devout young man, bearing the appropriate name of Cattolica, who without faltering kept the upper hand. Through most of the novel it appeared to be the puny and socially unacceptable Pulga, whom the narrator befriended and patronized. By the end of the story, however, the tables had been turned: Pulga had stabbed his benefactor in the back; the narrator, listening by invitation behind a door in Cattolica's house, had gone through the excruciating experience of hearing his adolescent confidences slyly mocked and, still worse, his own mother besmirched with vulgar sexual innuendo. He himself had proved unable to confront his traitorous friend; he had been obliged to recognize that it was Pulga, not he, who possessed sufficient worldly wisdom "to look . . . the whole truth . . . in the face."[39] The subsequent taste of enchantment, the reader was left to conclude, could never efface the darkness that had descended on his soul.

The atmosphere of *The Heron* was darker still. In this, the longest and most profound of his novellas, Bassani returned to third-person narration. No longer was it the narrative of an observer, as in his early stories of Ferrara; it was the day-long self-observation of a man without hope, the first and only one of the author's great "composed" characters into whose consciousness he permitted himself to peer. Here at last Bassani let a Jew who was manifestly not an emanation of his own person bare his inmost feelings—the feelings of a moral mediocrity, hurt, angry, and bewildered.

On a cold Sunday in late 1947 Edgardo Limentani drove off to the marshes of the Po to shoot birds, something he had not done for fifteen years. Why he did so was far from apparent, even to himself. Evidently it had some connection with a compulsion to reassert his prerogatives as a landowner, a rentier with property not on a Finzi-Contini scale but close to a thousand acres. (Like the physician-father of the narrator in *Behind the Door,* Limentani had a profession, in this case the law, which he scarcely practiced.) The previous April he had suffered a "nasty mishap": on a visit to his lands he had been surrounded by a group of militant peasants who with threats of physical violence had extracted from him a pledge to revise upward the sharecropping agreements under which they worked. After his return to Ferrara he had decided to renege on his promise; still more, he had denounced his rebellious tenants to the police. Since that date he had not dared set foot on the property which gave him status and for which he nourished inarticulate sentiments that might almost be called affection.[40]

Limentani had a further reason to go off hunting, a reason deriving likewise from shame. His family life no longer gave him pleasure—if it ever had—and a day in the open air might afford relief from the sullen atmosphere which enveloped him at home. He felt unable to love either his wife or his daughter—perhaps because both, like the concession made to his farmhands, had been forced on him by events that passed his understanding. Eight years earlier he had married his mistress, a non-Jew from a lower social order (echoes of David in the first of Bassani's stories and of Dr. Elia Corcos!)—a cool calculation, it would seem, to circumvent the anti-Semitic laws. Why else had Limentani transferred his property to his wife's name? Why else had he fled to Switzerland for the year and a half of German occupation?

An unheroic record, but not unusual in Italian Jewry's time of despair. Bassani appended no moralizing commentary; instead, he gave the whole matter a bitter ironic twist by contrasting it with the more thorough and consistent apostasy of Limentani's older cousin. This cousin had anticipated the coming persecution by more than a half-decade: in 1932 "he had suddenly decided to burn his bridges, marry an ordinary woman, the first within reach, be baptized, set up house and family in the plain; and disappear, practically speaking." His rupture with his coreligionists had been total and irrevocable. The woman he married had "made trousers" in Codigoro, the small town east of Ferrara where he had settled and which served as the point of departure for shooting expeditions to the marshes.[41] Her voice over the phone, at the end of a long and desolate day, was the only contact Limentani made with his cousin's family. The cousin himself never materialized; his example merely hovered in the background, potent and threatening through its very invisibility.

As for the shooting, it was a curiously mixed fiasco. Once arrived at his destination, Limentani found himself incapable of firing a single shot. He left that to his local guide, who deftly brought down more than forty birds. Among them was a heron—no good to eat, but when stuffed making "a fine ornament." As he watched the mortally wounded bird dragging itself about in an obstinate, baffled search for a refuge, Limentani first felt an impulse to put it out of its misery. Once more, however, he refrained from shooting. To have fired on the heron, he thought, in an initial glimpse of illumination, would have seemed like "shooting in a sense at himself." Yet "at least it would be all over."[42]

Back in Codigoro the illumination came in full flood. Tramping the streets in bewilderment, Limentani remembered the heron. It too had "felt . . . hemmed in on all sides, without the slightest possibility of escape. With this difference . . . to his disadvantage: that he was alive, quite alive." It was only a step, literally and in mental progression, to a taxidermist's shop window. Within lay magnificence —"silence, absolute stillness, peace." Gazing in fascination at the stuffed birds behind the glass, Limentani "felt slowly approaching . . . a secret thought that would free him." The birds, he now observed, were more beautiful by far "than when they were breathing and the blood ran swiftly through their veins": embalmed and mounted, they glowed with a "perfection of . . . beauty . . . , final and imperishable."[43]

So the story rushed to its close. At home he needed only to prepare his gun for the last act and to say good night to his mother—not to his wife or daughter. The mother thus singled out for his farewell was of course Jewish. And he seemed to derive satisfaction from recalling that he "had regularly paid the annual dues to the . . . community . . . No one . . . could raise any objections" to his burial in the Jewish cemetery."[44] It was as though his suicide might restore him, in a sense deeper than he could possibly think or express, to the company of his fellow-Jews. It was as though what remained of his Judaism could be saved through death alone.

"Only the dead are well off." In the last volume of his *Romanzo,* Bassani was to have the nine-year-old Bruno Lattes repeat at his grandfather's burial the words he had heard his father say at breakfast. The *Romanzo* was punctuated by evocations of funerals and cemeteries: it was permeated by a *vocazione mortuaria,* an imperative to come to terms with death.[45] For Bassani death figured as majestic: it opened the way to undimmed memory—just as the act of writing embalmed for eternity on the printed page the writer's reveries and recollections. In his own time Jews had been slaughtered by the millions. Through telling a few of their stories in a prose which itself had an unearthly quality of serene perfection, he might grant them an immortality they had deserved but mostly never sought. The greater part of Europe's Jews had perished; the least the survivors could do was to enshrine their memory in the splendor of art. Through such an act of piety Italian Judaism might continue to shine in the hearts of those whom death had spared and in the hearts of their descendants for generations to come.

The Cycle Closed

At first glance the concentration-camp veteran Geo Josz and the morose landowner Edgardo Limentani might seem to have little in common beyond their wealth and their Jewish origin. Yet with these, the only two of his major characters whom he situated in the postwar era, Bassani conveyed a similar message. Both longed in vain for the days before Fascism ostracized them; both found it impossible to reinsert themselves in the new society, even when it began to resemble the old. Limentani did not alter his resolve after his mother had reminded him in their final conversation "that political matters were taking a turn for the better"; Josz disappeared from Ferrara a half-year later, just at the moment of "normalization." It was as though the anti-Semitic laws were a "time bomb" whose delayed action could destroy even those who had apparently come through unscathed. It was as though in men such as Josz and Limentani "something essential" had been "dashed to pieces."[46]

The Italian world was *spezzato*—the violent expression Natalia Ginzburg used in telling what had happened to her after the death of Leone. Perhaps Bassani too felt a comparable explosion resound in his own soul. With *The Heron* he had reached the ultimate in desolation. In his final volume, published four years later in 1972, he simply tied up the loose ends of his *Romanzo,* inserting as its opening episode a marvelous "fairy tale" (of which more in my concluding remarks) and wryly questioning how someone who had grown up in Ferrara could ever manage to feel at ease in "the immense, shapeless cement hive" that Rome had become.[47]

The years in which Bassani completed the stories of his

native city and gave them their collective title were ones in which the public perspective on Jews began to shift decisively. For three decades, and for the first and only time, they had been at the center of modern history: from 1938—from Germany's *Kristallnacht,* which was almost exactly contemporaneous with Italy's official adoption of anti-Semitism—to the Six-Day War of 1967, the fate of the Jewish people had engaged the anguished sympathy of men and women of good will. It had stimulated a trio of young Italians to write *as Jews* of what they had seen or suffered or imagined. As the Western world entered the 1970s such memories began to recede into the stillness of a past that was closed and done with. The young people proclaimed their innocence of horrors in which they had not shared; their elders for the most part were only too happy to find a reason for shedding the sense of guilt, direct or vicarious, which had oppressed them for a quarter-century. A pretext lay ready to hand: first the Six-Day War, then the Yom Kippur War of 1973 (and the ensuing Arab oil embargo), cast the state of Israel in a new and unappealing role: not only had it become a nuisance in the conduct of ordinary living; it had changed from a refuge for the persecuted into a warrior nation which itself held down by force the discontented strangers within its swollen borders.

From this shift of sentiment of course a minority of non-Jews dissented. There were also Jews who nourished doubts about Israel's policy. For Natalia Ginzburg to "speak against" the Israelis was to offend her "own family." Yet she regretted that one could no longer imagine their country as "little" and"defenseless," a country in which each citizen "might preserve his own style, slight, bitter, reflective, and solitary"; she refused to share in the "admiration and devotion" they aroused in people of her own origin. Although she still thought of herself as Jewish—the "graver and more burdensome . . .part" of her mixed heritage—she no longer wrote of Jews.[48] She wrote as a woman who had reverted to the stance of detached observer to which she had clung before a flood of tenderness had engulfed her.

When in that same crucial year, 1973, she returned to the novel form, the book she published could be read as an answer to (or retraction of) her *Family Sayings* of a decade earlier.[49] *Dear Michele* depicted a family in full dissolution: far from sharing a private language, the voices of its members, apathetic and selfish, barely reached one another. They dwelt in a world of futility, the world of Alberto Moravia's *noia.* All along, while his juniors had listened to the call of ethnic solidarity, the mocking, profoundly wounded old Roman had continued to spin his tales of psychic dissociation. Perhaps in the end he had been proved right. Perhaps it was irrelevant to have been born a Jew.

There remained, however, the sense of "secret complicity" which Natalia Ginzburg experienced every time she discovered that someone else was Jewish.[50] There remained the "splendor" of memory she evoked on the last page of her novel. There remained the recognition of a claim to sympathy on the part of all the suffering, the universal claim of ecumenical humanism. By 1974, although the half-century of Italian Judaism's Silver Age might be over, the chain of recollection held firm.

6

The Meanings of "Survival"

"One of the most odious forms of anti-Semitism," Giorgio Bassani has written, is "to complain that Jews" are "not enough *like* other people, and then, . . . having ascertained their almost total assimilation . . . , to complain" of the opposite: that they are "the same as everyone else."[1] It would be wise to heed Bassani's implied warning to non-Jews in returning to the question posed at the start of this book: what is left of identity when language and religion are gone? The criteria of a minority's survival are manifold and difficult to assess with precision; they deserve a nuanced treatment at every stage.

By now it must be apparent that Italy's assimilated Jews, however they might strike others as "the same as everyone else," in their own view preserved something distinctive and precious. From the outside they passed unperceived as different; within they felt themselves to be special—although frequently in a half-conscious and inchoate fashion. We may recall the *private* character of Italian Judaism; we may recall the "secret complicity" that linked them one to another—an innocent complicity, one should add, since it carried no threat to those beyond the charmed circle. Composed of elements such as these, a residual ethnic consciousness maintained itself throughout what I have called their Silver Age and into the last quarter of the twentieth century.

❧

Much of the above might be said of Jews elsewhere in the Western world. Yet among communities of "survivors," Italy's manifested peculiarities that mirrored both its two-thousand-year tradition and the way it had emerged from the torment of the period 1938-1945. Its "remnant" was relatively large: compared to Eastern or Central European experience, or even to that of France, its sense of a living past was far more secure. If persecution and exile accelerated the withering of its small communities, by the same process they stimulated the regrouping and consolidation of those that remained. Italian Jewry returned to its origins: it fell back on its ancient stronghold in Rome. The move of leading writers from Turin or Ferrara to the capital paralleled a wider demographic shift. By the mid-1970s nearly half of Italy's 35,000 Jews were living in Rome; during the previous half-decade, two-thirds of the marriages celebrated throughout the country according to a Jewish rite had taken place there.[2]

With the establishment of the new state of Israel, for the first time in nearly two millennia Roman Jews experienced the exhilarating sense that there no longer remained any point in their city which was off limits to them—even if the place in question was small and its forbidden quality of their own devising. It is worth recording the symbolic event (one figuring rarely if at all in histories of contemporary Italy) that marked the change. On December 2, 1947, in celebration of Israel's declaration of independence, a crowd of more than a thousand gathered around the Arch of Titus. "From time immemorial, Jews had not walked *under* the Arch, which commemorated the destruction of the Temple and the humiliation of having been deported. Now, as though by a general tacit agreement, many . . . filed by *under* the Arch . . . ; the centuries-old vow" not to do so "had been annulled."[3]

Studying and writing in his prison cell, Antonio Gramsci happened upon a book review by a young scholar, Arnaldo Momigliano, who had before him more than a half-century of learned publication on Jewish and classical history alike. The Marxist theoretician concurred in Momigliano's explanation of the near-absence of Italian anti-Semitism. In Italy, they agreed, the formation of a national consciousness had not preceded the awakening of a similar Italian consciousness among the Jews; these had renounced their "particularism" at the same time as the majority of their countrymen. Something comparable, however, might have been said of Germany. What made Italy different, as Momigliano was to note nearly fifty years later, was that "the Jewish tradition" had formed "a component of Italian culture since the origins of Christianity . . . , and even earlier."[4]

Gramsci's words were written only a half-decade before anti-Semitism suddenly erupted in brutal exclusionary legislation—an event which he did not live to see. Had his health held out longer, he might have dismissed Mussolini's aberration as a mere "parenthesis" in a national experience which overall had been quite the contrary. Such too has been a basic assumption of this book: in modern Italy hatred of the Jews has been an anemic growth, without deep roots in popular sentiment.

How did matters look a generation after the time of torment came to an end? A survey, dating once more from the early 1970s, gives a firm basis for an assessment. A conscientious compendium and analysis of press statements, of polemical books and pamphlets, and of provocative incidents, it traces the Italian dimensions of late-twentieth-century anti-Semitism. From the mass of evidence presented, two generalizations emerge: after twenty years of relative quiet, the late 1960s witnessed a recrudescence of hostility to the Jews; this revival, however, was on a modest scale and contingent on events only tangentially related to Italian Judaism.[5]

Among the incidents recorded—for the most part the desecration of cemeteries and memorial plaques (but not of synagogues)—a few directly concerned the dramatis personae of our account. In 1966, and again in 1967, local vandals daubed a swastika on the plaque honoring the Pisan parnas, Giuseppe Pardo Roques. A few years later similar markings were twice discovered on the plaque in Ferrara which had roused the indignation of the fictional concentration-camp survivor Geo Josz—a plaque, incidently, bearing the names of four members of the Bassani family. Increasingly such graffiti included slogans condemning Israel and extolling the deeds of the Palestine Liberation Organization, unmistakable testimony to the impingement of events beyond Italy's borders.

Meantime a minority of Catholic publications were seeking to reawaken a long-dormant religious antagonism. The pretext was once again extra- or supra-Italian: the Church universal at the Second Vatican Council had shocked theological conservatives by absolving the Jews from the age-old charge of deicide; the response of local scribblers was to disinter the whole baggage of anti-Semitic folklore. This kind of polemic was bound eventually to subside. With the death or retirement of ecclesiastical diehards Italy, at least as well as other countries, could settle into a post-Conciliar mood of mutual religious acceptance. Sympathy for the PLO was less likely to go away; it continued to be fed by military action in which Israelis often appeared the aggressors. The Communist elder statesman, senator-for-life, *and* Jew Umberto Terracini tried to put the best face on the matter: Jews were resorting to warlike responses, thereby "inevitably arousing . . . the aversion that the Italian popular masses" had "always manifested . . . for wars."[6] Terracini might have added that it was the PLO which had initiated the cycle of violence.

All things considered, however, there was little evidence that by the mid-1970s, Italy's Jews felt personally threatened or denied public acceptance. The vast majority believed it possible to live at peace in their own country; they felt no compulsion to emigrate to Israel.[7] It is instructive to compare these findings with a similar, if more impressionistic, survey published in France six years later. Such a comparison needs to take account of basic historical differences in the situation of Jews in two democracies, Latin, Catholic, and tolerant, which at first might seem much the same. In France modern anti-Semitism has been more vigorous and tenacious than in Italy: we may recall the vast discrepancy in emotional intensity between the late-nineteenth-century case of Senator Maurogonato and that of Captain Dreyfus; we may recall the relative "moderation" of Italian Fascism as against the virulence of the Vichy regime, and the protection extended to Jews by the Italians in the southeastern zone of France they occupied from November 1942 until the following September—a protection which "irritated" Pétain's henchmen.[8] Perhaps most of all we should bear in mind the fact that France's Jewish minority had always been larger than Italy's, that by the 1970s it had grown to nearly twenty times the size of the Italian, and that at least two-thirds of this increase had resulted from a flood of new arrivals from North Africa.

Which is all to say that, by the time of the survey in question, French Jewry was far more visible, far less homogeneous and assimilated, than Italian. It is perhaps not surprising, then, that for the most part those interviewed should have voiced a feeling of insecurity almost totally lacking in Italy. What was striking nevertheless was the vivid, frequently violent language—"three synagogues are burning"—in which they conveyed their sense of a "low, dull threat, latent but unremitting," and their conviction (usually platonic) that one would be well-advised to depart for Israel. In a word, France's Jews described themselves as "embarrassing" to their countrymen; Italy's did not.[9]

If the emotional climate in the country which geographically and ideologically might appear closest to Italy emerges as notably dissimilar, we are back to the notion of the uniqueness of Italian Jewry. It was not a community swollen beyond recognition, such as that of France. It was not a community reduced to a pathetic handful of survivors, such as those of Central and Eastern Europe. It was a small but quietly assured community, at ease with itself and with its non-Jewish neighbors. It had always been the oldest such community in the Western world; with the massive absorption of Middle Eastern Jews into Israel, it had become the oldest in the entire diaspora.

The criteria of survival examined thus far have been approximate and tangible. They have referred primarily to the observant or to those explicitly affiliated with organized Judaism. What can one say of the unobservant and those who scarcely if ever entered a temple? On Jews of this sort statistics are fragmentary or nonexistent; *their* residual loyalty to Judaism has left few traces. Yet these have been the subjects of our investigation—the writers, the intellectuals, whose spiritual affinity with their tradition and with one another for the most part remained invisible. What have we learned of a second and more subtle meaning of the word survival? What has literature taught us or illuminated about family resemblances, about a submerged thread of shared sensibility? How much of what we have managed to bring to the surface or decipher bears the mark of a cherished legacy from a very ancient past?

Undoubtedly the experience of persecution, in Italy as elsewhere, acted as a powerful stimulant in reviving the consciousness of that legacy. We have seen it at work, notably in the case of Natalia Ginzburg. But this was only half the story: in Italy the emotional material for such a revival was already at hand; even in our highly assimilated protagonists a slender thread of memory reached back to a rich oral tradition. Perhaps it was for this reason that the Jewish "voice" did not fall silent in the post-Second World War years—that the "presence" of writers of Jewish origin was more perceptible there than in any other European country.

The last chapter broke off at the empty spiritual world of Edgardo Limentani, and along with it the implication that Limentani's bleak view of the universe had virtually obliterated the restrained but tenacious trust in the future epitomized by the "secret plan" of Ermanno Finzi-Contini. Had their creator left the matter there, little more would remain to be said. But Bassani had something further to impart. Once again he seemed to be rectifying what he had written in an earlier work. As the opening episode in the last volume of his *Romanzo*—and in so meticulous a writer as Bassani this prominent position could not have been accidental—he composed a self-styled "fairy tale" entitled "Necessity Is the Veil of God."

The story, a scant six pages long, was among the most lyric he had ever written. It concerned a young woman of Ferrara, a woman with "sad, . . . Sephardic eyes," devoted to her aged parents, who had rejected every suitor whom the customary network of relatives and intermediaries had proposed. Finally, in the ripeness of her early thirties, she had chosen quite on her own the most unlikely candidate, a Ukrainian six years her junior. He had arrived from Odessa unannounced, and with his mother and father had stayed on as "guests" of the Ferrarese Jewish community. All three had been deported during the war: their names had been inscribed on the celebrated commemorative plaque. But before disappearing the young Ashkenazi had begotten a son, an event which had been his wife's true purpose all along. And the resolve to bring a child into the world had certainly "been worth it." The baby proved exceptional in every way: "intelligent, lively, . . . very handsome . . . , so . . . that to the few of us who escaped the extermination camps and the rest, when, in 1945, the men no longer separated from the women, we were all together" in one "synagogue, the boy seemed the very personification of life that eternally ends and eternally begins again."[10]

So one might hazard the guess that at long last Bassani too had become a "prisoner of hope." In his case "prisoner" may be precisely the right word. Despite his apparent pessimism, despite his celebration of death, he had discovered no alternative to trust in an uncertain future; the serene lyricism of his literary style conveyed as much, even when the ostensible matter at hand might be profoundly depressing. To be captive to one's hope bore a close relation to cherishing one's memories; it suggested a capacity to transmute even the worst of those recollections into what Primo Levi called a "treasure." For if he, in common with his namesake Carlo, managed to extract "poetry" from the trials they had undergone—if both wrote with an undercurrent of irrepressible joy—it was perhaps because those very sufferings had furnished them with a shield against despair, had endowed them with something approaching a conviction that the evils the future was bound to bring could likewise be surmounted. "The dear, the sweet . . . past," as Micòl Finzi-Contini expressed it, figured as far more ambiguous than a repository for what was serene and protected; her own future, in common with that of so many of her coreligionists, was to be annihilation. The fictional Micòl, like her age-mate the real Natalia, found herself obliged to have recourse again and again to the protective distancing from horror which irony bestowed. Yet the irony of their generation—and here the attributes of imaginary characters and those of their creators blend—was seldom bitter; it was rather the wry smile of men and women who have seen through the grosser forms of illusion but hold on to the "little margin" indispensable for survival.

The eternal hope of a people whose sufferings have likewise been eternal, this echo has emerged as our overarching theme. What of the others that we have identified along the way?

1. In the work of the younger generation of writers, the holocaust generation, *senilità* was left behind. Of necessity their own lives and commitments had been too strenuous to allow for the self-indulgence of imagining themselves as prematurely worn-out. They had gained the resourcefulness—one thinks again of Primo Levi and Natalia Ginzburg—for slow but certain reengagement in life after unimaginable disaster. To be a Jew had proved far more painful than their childhoods had led them to believe; at the same time, they had escaped the world-weariness so often associated with a lack of clear identity. Traces of *senilità* might linger in Bassani's

elegiac mode; for the most part it had receded into the twilight of an obscure temptation bequeathed by earlier generations, a temptation against which the writer needed to be constantly on guard.

2. It would be idle to recapitulate how often we have encountered the theme of exile—whether in emigration, in hiding, in enforced residence, or in camps of extermination. It would be just as superfluous to stress its familiarly Jewish character. What we need to underline is its variant: the feeling of exclusion or ostracism that Bassani found "atrocious." A peculiarly acute sense of exile struck sensitive, highly assimilated young Italians with the shock of the unbelievable. In this respect their experience was worse than that of coreligionists elsewhere who had suspected all along that something of the sort might one day befall them. In Italy an ingrained reluctance to recognize the blunt fact of exclusion recalled how Jews of the sixteenth century, accepted and even esteemed by their neighbors, must have felt when they awoke to find themselves being herded into ghettos. Peculiar to Italy also was the stubborn conviction that ostracism could be only temporary, that sooner or later their countrymen would return to their senses. Here, as nearly everywhere else, it might be the Jews' fate to suffer from time to time under an ancestral curse; it was also the Italian Jews' good fortune—denied to so many others—to succeed in rejoining the national community. This too gave the younger writers the inner confidence to tell of what they had endured with a surprising lack of bitterness.

3. As for the family—what more Jewish (or Italian) a theme! The veil of tenderness that enveloped so much of the work we have reviewed, a tenderness that hovered over it even when the writer intended quite otherwise, derived in

great part from memories of home. Yet in what may seem the most banal of literary material we have detected a Jewish variant of an Italian norm. The home, the family, has figured not only as a consortium for mutual defense; it has figured as a moral base where parents and children could cherish the same civic values and face a hostile world with the reassurance of ideological solidarity, where private and public concerns were of a piece. On fretful fledgling literati, family ties may have originally acted as a constraint: when the shared necessity of standing up to oppression began to grip each family, petty generational differences sank into irrelevance, and the strength which came from remembered affection took their place.

That strength combined gentleness with a self-imposed moral severity—qualities seldom joined one to another. The severity derived from a familiar Jewish source: The Law. Even in sophisticated late-twentieth-century Jews who had renounced formal observances, the sense of a moral imperative could remain "intact" as a "secret patrimony of the spirit, an invisible guide to action."[11] In a national community which by its own admission was riddled with moral laxity on all levels Jews could seem different, to themselves and to others, by their more rigorous standards of personal and civic conduct. Such standards the fictional Limentani notably lacked. Perhaps it was for this reason that "something essential" within him had been "dashed to pieces."

Respect for ethical tradition did not imply a readiness to condemn outsiders—quite the contrary. Again and again in the course of this study we have remarked on a reluctance on the part of individual Jews or their literary creations to sit in judgment: we may recall Primo Levi's openness of mind toward his Russian hosts and his refusal to hate the Germans as a people; we may recall the shame of the narrator in *The Gold-rimmed Eyeglasses* when he felt a loathing for what was "*goyish*" welling up in his soul. The absence of provincialism, the "freedom of judgment," that Norberto Bobbio found in his young Torinesi friends would have been incompatible with a conviction of being the sole custodians of moral truth. The Jews of Italy might hold it in special esteem, but they claimed no monopoly of virtue.

For that, they had lived for too many generations alongside Christians; their lives had been too closely entangled with those of their Catholic neighbors. The process of mutual interpenetration between the two faiths—although scarcely recognized by either—for two millennia had done its silent work: a "Roman" Catholicism and a "Roman" Judaism shared more than they knew. It is worth remembering that it was in Rome on a Sabbath night of October 1943 that Italian non-Jews on a large scale first showed themselves "truly Christians" by giving asylum to the panic-stricken victims of a mass roundup. A nontheological ecumenicism was already in existence long before the Second Vatican Council gave it official sanction. "His thought frequently went out toward the Christians," a descendant has written of the father of Isacco Artom, the first of Italy's great Jewish statesmen, "toward Jesus, who he knew had sprung from his own people and had been nourished by the same Law—a Law which he had preached, inviting all human beings to love one another."[12]

We are back to the all-embracing theme of hope—and this last time with a specification of the hope on which men and women of Jewish origin gladly acknowledged their dependence. It found its clearest expression in the "ecumenical-humanist-progressive" mentality sketched at the start of this book, a mentality of openness toward non-Jews, permissive and secular. It sought reconciliation and mutual respect between people whom the religious antagonisms of the past had kept apart; it aspired toward a world at peace. "The world is not friendly," the parnas of Pisa is supposed to have said. *"We have to make it friendly;* it is up to us."[13] The mentality embodied in words such as these was the reverse of a focus on Jewish particularism; it implied a steady widening of one's range of sympathy.

Thus, in a continuing course of self-definition, a definition spontaneously chosen rather than one imposed by outsiders, what was explicitly and historically Jewish became absorbed in, and by the same process infused, moral and aesthetic material derived from the non-Jewish and/or secular universe. With this recognition one reaches the ultimate paradox of Jewish allegiance in an intellectual and nonobservant Italian context. The restraints, the narrowing, that once had given reason for casting off the identification had ceased to operate. The opposite was true: the yearning for what was universal acted as a powerful incentive for retaining it.

As early as the Jewish youth meeting of 1924 Nello Rosselli had explained with passionate conviction how his spirit was sustained by a sense of his own Judaism which was both personal and widespread. He freely confessed that he did not go to temple, that he knew no Hebrew, that he observed no ritual practices. Yet he "held on" to his Jewish identity for reasons which he found amply sufficient. Among them he gave high rank to its ethical severity and its "religious sense of the family." Above all else, however, he regarded himself as still a Jew because he loved "all men as in Israel we are commanded to love" them. Or rather, he added, and this was the crux of the matter, because "we cannot help but love" them.[14]

Notes

Chapter 1. The Most Ancient of Minorities

1. Notably Cecil Roth, whose *The History of the Jews of Italy* (Philadelphia: Jewish Publication Society of America, 1946) is the older standard account, and Attilio Milano, whose *Storia degli ebrei in Italia* (Turin: Einaudi, 1963) is more comprehensive and furnishes a fuller scholarly apparatus.

2. Sergio Della Pergola, *Anatomia dell' ebraismo italiano* (Assisi and Rome: Beniamino Carucci, 1976), p. 253. This is the indispensable sociological and demographic guide.

3. Giorgio Bassani, *Dietro la porta* (Turin: Einaudi, 1964), tr. William Weaver, *Behind the Door* (New York: Harcourt Brace Jovanovich, 1972), pp. 31–32.

4. See the roster of "notables in the intellectual field" in Guido Bedarida's *Ebrei d'Italia* (Livorno: Società Editrice Tirrena, 1950), p. 104. Besides the names of Ascoli, D'Ancona, and Franchetti, known "throughout Italy," Bedarida lists for Piedmont: Artom, Debenedetti, Foà, Fubini, Momigliano, Ottolenghi, Segre; for Lombardy: Fano, Mortara; for Venetia: Errera, Gentilli, Luzzatti-o, Morpurgo, Musatti, Pincherle; for Emilia and Romagna: Delvecchio, Donati, Finzi; for Tuscany: Supino.

5. Roth, *Jews of Italy,* pp. 407, 419–420.

6. Milano, *Ebrei in Italia,* pp. 535, 537–538.

7. Ibid., pp. 572–576; see also Lea Scazzocchio Sestieri, "Sulla

parlata Giudaico-Romanesca," in Daniel Carpi, Attilio Milano, Umberto Nahon, eds., *Scritti in memoria di Enzo Sereni* (Milan and Jerusalem: Fondazione Sally Mayer, 1970), pp. 101–132.

8. Roth, *Jews of Italy,* p. 492.

9. Milano, *Ebrei in Italia,* p. 374.

10. Bedarida, *Ebrei d'Italia,* p. 216; Andrew M. Canepa, "Cattolici ed ebrei nell' Italia liberale (1870–1915)," *Comunità*, 32 (April 1978), 107.

11. Renzo De Felice, *Storia degli ebrei italiani sotto il fascismo,* 3rd ed. (Turin: Einaudi, 1972), pp. 465–467.

12. Augusto Segre, *Memorie di vita ebraica: Casale Monferrato – Roma – Gerusalemme, 1918–1960* (Rome: Bonacci, 1979), p.126.

13. Milano, *Ebrei in Italia,* pp. 458, 694.

14. Della Pergola, *Anatomia dell'ebraismo,* pp. 53–55; Carlo M. Cipolla, *Before the Industrial Revolution: European Society and Economy, 1000–1700,* 2nd ed. (New York and London: Norton, 1980), p. 4.

15. Milano, *Ebrei in Italia,* pp. 679–680; Roth, *Jews of Italy,* pp. 193–215; Hermann Vogelstein, *Rome* (in Jewish Communities series), tr. Moses Hadas (Philadelphia: Jewish Publication Society of America, 1941), pp. 221–226, 253–255.

16. Della Pergola, *Anatomia dell'ebraismo,* pp. 254, 264; cf. Bedarida, *Ebrei d'Italia,* p. 266.

17. Milano, *Ebrei in Italia,* p. 355.

18. Quoted in Andrew M. Canepa, "Emancipazione, integrazione e antisemitismo liberale in Italia: il caso Pasqualigo," *Comunità*, 29 (June 1975), 193.

19. Bedarida's *Ebrei d'Italia* offers a conscientious roster, esp. pp. 188–189, 217–219, 230.

20. Canepa, "Cattolici ed ebrei," pp. 89–91.

21. On all the foregoing, see Delio Cantimori's preface to De Felice's *Ebrei italiani sotto il fascismo,* pp. xviii–xx, and the fuller account in Canepa, "Il caso Pasqualigo," pp. 166–169, 177, 190.

22. Canepa, "Cattolici ed ebrei," pp. 107–109.

23. For the former contention, see ibid., pp. 45–48; for the latter, see De Felice, *Ebrei italiani sotto il fascismo,* pp. 13, 21.

24. Segre, *Memorie,* pp. 31, 42, 50; Bedarida, *Ebrei d'Italia,* p. 266.

25. For accounts of the meeting, see De Felice, *Ebrei italiani sotto il fascismo,* pp. 88–92, and Ruth Bondy, *The Emissary: A Life of Enzo Sereni,* tr. Shlomo Katz (Boston and Toronto: Little, Brown, 1977), pp. 52–53.

26. Milano, *Ebrei in Italia,* pp. 370, 693; Roth, *Jews of Italy,* p. 475. The whole passage is characteristic of a learned and deeply humane scholar's optimistic outlook, which, in view of Canepa's subsequent researches, requires some darker shading.

27. Giorgio Romano, "L'elemento ebraico in romanzi di scrittori ebrei italiani," in Daniel Carpi, Attilio Milano, Alexander Rofé, eds., *Scritti in memoria di Leone Carpi* (Milan and Jerusalem: Fondazione Sally Mayer, 1967), p. 187.

28. Ibid., p. 207.

29. De Felice, *Ebrei italiani sotto il fascismo,* p. 17; Della Pergola, *Anatomia dell'ebraismo,* p.115.

30. Ludwig Wittgenstein, *Philosophische Untersuchungen,* tr. G. E. M. Anscombe, *Philosophical Investigations,* 3rd ed. (New York: Macmillan, 1958), ¶ 67.

Chapter 2. Exercises in Futility: Trieste and Rome

1. Italo Svevo, "Profilo autobiografico," in *Racconti – Saggi – Pagine sparse (Opera Omnia,* III) (Milan: Dall'Oglio, 1968), p. 801.

2. On Weiss and the Triestino psychoanalytic circle, see Michel David, *La psicoanalisi nella cultura italiana* (Turin: Boringhieri, 1966), pp. 199–200, 373–375, 379.

3. Umberto Saba, preface (1952) to "Gli Ebrei: Trieste, 1910–1912," in *Prose (Opere,* I) (Milan: Mondadori, 1964), pp. 10–12.

4. Hermann Vogelstein, *Rome* (in Jewish Communities series), tr. Moses Hadas (Philadelphia: Jewish Publication Society of America, 1941), pp. 350–352; Bruno Di Porto, "Gli ebrei di Roma dai Papi all'Italia", in Elio Toaff et al., *1870: La breccia del ghetto: Evoluzione degli ebrei di Roma* (Rome: Barulli, 1971), pp. 17–78.

5. Giuliana Piperno Beer, "Gli ebrei di Roma nel passaggio dal Governo Pontificio allo Stato Liberale Italiano," in *La breccia del ghetto,* pp. 184–187.

6. On the new synagogue, see Attilio Milano, *Storia degli ebrei in Italia* (Turin: Einaudi, 1963), p. 450, and Vogelstein, *Rome,* pp. 370–371.

7. Augusto Segre, *Memorie di vita ebraica: Casale Monferrato – Roma – Gerusalemme, 1918–1960* (Rome: Bonacci, 1979), p. 172.

8. Piperno Beer, "Gli ebrei di Roma," pp. 160–161; Ruth Bondy, *The Emissary: A Life of Enzo Sereni,* tr. Shlomo Katz (Boston and Toronto: Little, Brown, 1977), pp. 3–7.

9. Piperno Beer, "Gli ebrei di Roma," pp. 161, 169.

10. Introduction by Bruno Maier to Italo Svevo, *Romanzi (Opera Omnia,* II) (Milan: Dall'Oglio, 1969), pp. 14–15, 38–41.

11. Giacomo Debenedetti, "Lettera a Carocci" (1929), in *Saggi critici: Seconda serie (Opere,* II) (Milan: Il Saggiatore, 1971), p. 93; Sergio Solmi, "Ricordo di Svevo," in *Omaggio a Italo Svevo* (special number of the review *Solariä),* no. 3–4 (1929), p. 71.

12. Svevo, "Profilo autobiografico," p. 799.

13. Bruno Maier, ed., *Lettere a Svevo/Diario di Elio Schmitz* (Milan: Dall'Oglio, 1973), e.g., pp. 197, 198, 200, 221, 236–237.

14. In three studies of Svevo in English the following passages deal with Jewish associations: P. N. Furbank, *Italo Svevo: The Man and the Writer* (London: Secker & Warburg, 1966), pp. 3–11, 38, 43, 50–51, 96–99; Naomi Lebowitz, *Italo Svevo* (New Brunswick, N.J.: Rutgers University Press, 1978), pp. 39–40; Brian Moloney, *Italo Svevo: A Critical Introduction* (Edinburgh: Edinburgh University Press, 1974), pp. 1–3.

15. Saba, "Italo Svevo all'Ammiragliato britannico," in *Prose,* pp. 152–154.

16. Richard Ellmann, *James Joyce* (New York: Oxford University Press, 1969), p. 385. See also Furbank, *Svevo,* pp. 89–91.

17. "Shylock" (1880) is republished in *Opera Omnia,* III, 557–558.

18. Debenedetti, "Svevo e Schmitz" (1929), in *Saggi critici: Seconda serie*, pp. 57, 72, 83, 86, 89, 90.

19. Italo Svevo, *La coscienza di Zeno* (*Opera Omnia*, II), tr. Beryl de Zoete, *The Confessions of Zeno* (New York: Vintage, 1958), pp. 9–10, 28, 53, 248, 382.

20. Furbank in his *Svevo* agrees; pp. 183–184, 186.

21. For a summary statement, see David, *La psicoanalisi nella cultura italiana*, p. 385.

22. Alberto Moravia, "Nella condizione di natura," *La difesa della razza* (special number of the review *Il Ponte*), 34 (November 30–December 31, 1978), 1350–1351.

23. Jean Duflot, *Entretiens avec Alberto Moravia* (Paris: Pierre Belfond, 1970), pp. 10–11; Enzo Siciliano, *Moravia* (Milan: Longanesi, 1971), p. 55. Of the numerous extended interviews with Moravia, these are the two I have found most useful. See also the "Autobiografia in breve" in Roberto Tessari, *Alberto Moravia* (Florence: Le Monnier, 1975), pp. 1–5.

24. Duflot, *Entretiens*, pp. 12–13; Siciliano, *Moravia*, pp. 23–29.

25. Moravia included "Inverno di malato" (1930) in his first volume of short stories, *La bella vita* (1935).

26. Duflot, *Entretiens*, pp. 9, 17.

27. Ibid., p. 163. *La noia* (Milan: Bompiani, 1960) has been translated by Angus Davidson as *The Empty Canvas* (New York: Farrar, Straus & Cudahy, 1961).

28. Duflot, *Entretiens*, p. 90; Siciliano, *Moravia*, pp. 82–84.

29. Italo Svevo, *Senilità* (*Opera Omnia*, II), tr. Beryl de Zoete, *As a Man Grows Older* (New York: New Directions, 1949; for once the title in translation is more appropriate than the original), p. 244; Alberto Moravia, *Gli indifferenti*, reissued as vol. I of his *Opere complete* (Milan: Bompiani, 1978), tr. Angus Davidson, *The Time of Indifference* (Westport, Conn.: Greenwood, 1975), p. 302.

30. David, *La psicoanalisi nella cultura italiana*, p. 495.

31. Alberto Moravia, *Agostino*, tr. Beryl de Zoete, in *Two Adolescents* (New York: Farrar, Straus, 1950), pp. 109–110.

32. Alberto Moravia, *La disubbidienza*, tr. Angus Davidson,

Luca, in *Two Adolescents*, pp. 124, 127, 134, 135, 193, 260–261, 266–267.

33. David, *La psicoanalisi nella cultura italiana*, pp. 496, 498.

34. Such despondency was not of course a Jewish monopoly. It echoes throughout post-Romantic European literature—in Russia, —in France, in Germany. The theme of a weary ineptitude did not derive solely from life. It derived also from reading: the influence on Svevo of Gustave Flaubert's *Sentimental Education* is too familiar to require comment. Bassani as a young man also read Flaubert, and along with him a novelist of a later period and less well known in Italy, Theodor Fontane (who was in fact Flaubert's slightly older contemporary, although his last book did not appear until the very end of the century, in the same year as Svevo's *Senilità*). Where Flaubert vented the spleen of a lifetime's disappointment, Fontane laced his prose with urbane, tolerant humor about the ironies of life. Among these ironies was the curious fact that his audience largely consisted not of the Prussian aristocrats of whom he wrote but of a devoted circle of Jewish readers: Ernest K. Bramsted, *Aristocracy and the Middle-Classes in Germany: Social Types in German Literature 1830–1900*, rev ed. (Chicago: University of Chicago Press, 1964), pp. 262–268. Perhaps this was a case of elective affinity; certainly Fontane's self-disparaging irony and Svevo's bore a family resemblance. More generally the Italian Jewish variant on the common theme of *senilità* may be found (with the notable exception of Moravia) in a gradual passage from desperation to a tenuous hope.

35. The passages in question are from the *Purgatorio*, Canto V, lines 85–129, and from the *Inferno*, Canto XXVI, lines 85–142.

Chapter 3. Two Captives Called Levi

1. Renzo De Felice, *Storia degli ebrei italiani sotto il fascismo*, 3rd ed. (Turin: Einaudi, 1972), pp. 73–74. On Carlo Rosselli, see Aldo Garosci, *La Vita di Carlo Rosselli*, 2 vols. (Rome: Edizioni U, 1946), and *Storia dei fuorusciti* (Bari: Laterza, 1953), chs. 3, 5; on

Nello, see Zeffiro Ciuffoletti, "Nello Rosselli: A Historian under Fascism," *The Journal of Italian History*, 1 (Autumn 1978), 287–314. On Moravia's relations with his Rosselli cousins, see Enzo Siciliano, *Moravia* (Milan: Longanesi, 1971), pp. 26, 36.

2. Meir Michaelis, *Mussolini and the Jews: German-Italian Relations and the Jewish Question in Italy, 1922–1945* (Oxford: Clarendon, 1978), pp. 10–11, 30, 33, 69, 83, 410–412. With its wider documentation and focus on the international aspects of the question, this work supplements rather than supersedes that of De Felice, which remains basic to an understanding of the vicissitudes of the Jews within Italy itself. See the review by Arnaldo Momigliano in *The Journal of Modern History*, 52 (June 1980), 282–284.

3. De Felice (p. 243) and Michaelis (pp. vii, 126–127, 190) agree, as does the author of the older authoritative biography of Mussolini in English: Ivone Kirkpatrick, *Mussolini: A Study in Power* (New York: Hawthorn, 1964), p. 372.

4. De Felice, *Ebrei italiani sotto il fascismo*, pp. 219, 249, 252.

5. On the attitude of the House of Savoy, see Cecil Roth, *The History of the Jews of Italy* (Philadelphia: Jewish Publication Society of America, 1946), p. 479; on King and Pope, see De Felice, *Ebrei italiani sotto il fascismo*, pp. 284, 287–288.

6. Michaelis, *Mussolini and the Jews*, p. 239.

7. On DELASEM, the Jewish self-help organization that managed such departures, see De Felice, *Ebrei italiani sotto il fascismo*, pp. 416–417, and Augusto Segre, *Memorie di vita ebraica: Casale Monferrato – Roma – Gerusalemme, 1918–1960* (Rome: Bonacci, 1979), ch. 17.

8. On Pétain's regime, see Michael R. Marrus and Robert O. Paxton, *Vichy France and the Jews, 1940–44* (New York: Basic Books, 1981). See also André Harris and Alain de Sédouy, *Juifs et Français* (Paris: Grasset, 1979), pp. 85, 116–117.

9. Michaelis, *Mussolini and the Jews*, pp. 351, 413–414. De Felice (pp. 434, 448), is in substantial agreement. For a more severe verdict, see Giuseppe Mayda, "La persecuzione antisemita, 1943–

1945," *La difesa della razza* (special number of the review *Il Ponte*), 34 (November 30 – December 31, 1978), 1438–1439.

10. *L'Osservatore Romano*, October 25–26, 1943, quoted in Saul Friedländer, *Pie XII et le III*[e] *Reich, Documents* (Paris: Editions du Seuil, 1964), tr. Charles Fullman, *Pius XII and the Third Reich: A Documentation* (New York: Knopf, 1966), p. 208 (author's italics). For a magisterial assessment of Pius XII pro and con, see Michaelis, *Mussolini and the Jews*, pp. 372–377.

11. The figures are a composite of those furnished by De Felice (p. 453), Michaelis (pp. 389–392, 414), and Sergio Della Pergola, *Anatomia dell' ebraismo italiano* (Assisi and Rome: Beniamino Carucci, 1976), pp. 54, 143. Discrepancies arise from the method of counting converts to Christianity. For a comparative assessment of Jews saved in individual countries, see Helen Fein, *Accounting for Genocide: National Responses and Jewish Victimization during the Holocaust* (New York: Free Press, 1979), ch. 3.

12. Michaelis, *Mussolini and the Jews*, p. 367.

13. The anecdote is from Davide Lajolo, *Veder l'erba dalla parte delle radici* (Milan: Rissoli, 1977), p. 146; the concluding words from De Felice, *Ebrei italiani sotto il fascismo*, p. 469.

14. Laura Fermi, *Illustrious Immigrants: The Intellectual Migration from Europe, 1930–41* (Chicago: University of Chicago Press, 1968), pp. 120–122.

15. Michaelis, *Mussolini and the Jews*, p. 388. On the Sereni brothers, see Ruth Bondy, *The Emissary: A Life of Enzo Sereni*, tr. Shlomo Katz (Boston and Toronto: Little, Brown, 1977), and such standard histories of the Resistance as Roberto Battaglia, *Storia della resistenza italiana*, new ed. (Turin: Einaudi, 1970), pp. 210n, 540n, 575n, 642, Charles F. Delzell, *Mussolini's Enemies: The Italian Anti-Fascist Resistance* (Princeton: Princeton University Press, 1961), pp. 125, 356, 522–527, 539, and Max Salvadori, *Breve storia della Resistenza italiana* (Florence: Vallecchi, 1974), pp. 126, 159, 234.

16. For biographical details, see Mario Miccinesi, *Invito alla lettura di Carlo Levi*, 3rd. ed. (Milan: Mursia, 1977), ch. 1. For an overview of Levi as a painter, see *Carlo Levi: Mostra Antologica* (Milan: Electa, 1974).

17. Carlo Levi, *L'orologio* (Turin: Einaudi, 1950), tr. *The Watch* (New York: Farrar, Straus & Young, 1951), pp. 159–160, 238–240.

18. Carlo Levi, "Saba e il mondo ebraico," lecture to a Jewish youth group delivered in December 1957, in Gigliola De Donato, ed., *Coraggio dei miti: Scritti contemporanei, 1922–1974* (Bari: De Donato, 1975), p. 227–230, 240.

19. Carlo Levi, *Cristo si è fermato a Eboli* (Turin: Einaudi, 1945), tr. Frances Frenaye, *Christ Stopped at Eboli* (New York: Farrar, Straus, 1947), p. 3.

20. Ibid., p. 77.

21. Ibid., pp. 225, 228. I have altered the translation.

22. For the full meaning of this passage, one must return to the Italian original, p. 214.

23. Silvano Arieti, *The Parnas* (New York: Basic Books, 1979).

24. Lajolo, *Veder l'erba*, p. 123.

25. Primo Levi, *Il sistema periodico* (Turin: Einaudi, 1975), pp. 23–24, 43–44, 72, 207; Fiora Vincenti, *Invito alla lettura di Primo Levi* (Milan: Mursia, 1973), pp. 38, 54.

26. P. Levi, *Sistema periodico*, pp. 34, 37, 41–42, 47, 50.

27. Ibid., pp. 55–56.

28. Ibid., pp. 53, 133–134, 138.

29. Vincenti, *Invito alla lettura di Primo Levi*, pp. 55–56.

30. Primo Levi, *Se questo è un uomo* (Turin: Einaudi, 1958), pp. 7–8. These prefatory remarks are lacking in the translation by Stuart Woolf: *Survival in Auschwitz* (New York: Collier, 1961). See also Giorgio Romano, "La persecuzione e le deportazioni degli ebrei di Roma e d'Italia nelle opere di scrittori ebrei," in Daniel Carpi, Attilio Milano, Umberto Nahon, eds., *Scritti in memoria di Enzo Sereni* (Milan and Jerusalem: Fondazione Sally Mayer, 1970), p. 327.

31. P. Levi, *Survival in Auschwitz*, p. 156.

32. Ibid., pp. 135–136.

33. Ibid., p. 118. I have altered the translation.

34. Ibid., pp. 43, 54, 72.

35. P. Levi, *Sistema periodico*, pp. 215–228. A German translation

of this episode has been published in *Die Zeit*, 34 (July 6, 1979), 22–23.

36. Vincenti, *Invito alla lettura di Primo Levi*, pp. 102–103; Primo Levi, *La tregua* (Turin: Einaudi, 1963), tr. Stuart Woolf, *The Reawakening* (Boston and Toronto: Little, Brown, 1965), pp. 12, 191, 220.

37. Ibid., pp. 84, 117–118.

38. Ibid., pp. 59, 122, 126–127, 161–162.

39. Ibid., pp. 189–190.

40. Ibid., p. 13; P. Levi, *Sistema periodico*, p. 158. In the late 1970s and early 1980s Levi returned to the scenes of his first two books, with the initial section (entitled "Passato prossimo") of his *Lilít e altri racconti* (Turin: Einaudi, 1981) and with *Se non ora, quando?* (Turin: Einaudi, 1982). The first merely added a few new episodes previously published in periodicals. The second (with its title derived from Rabbi Hillel) was a novel of adventure which enjoyed a considerable public success and which marked a departure from the author's earlier work, since it dealt not with Italian Jewry, but with the long march of a partisan band of Russian and Polish Jews from Byelorussia to Milan—the *trampolino* for their goal of Palestine. This time, as he readily granted, Levi had been obliged "to reconstruct an era, a scenario, and a language [Yiddish]" which he "knew only spottily"—and beyond that, to evoke what was "surreal and subtle" in the "wild-eyed world of Ashkenazi Judaism" (pp. 78, 261–262). The result necessarily lacked the immediacy of his own reminiscences, although it added a number of elements that had scarcely figured there, notably a stress on Russian anti-Semitism.

41. Arieti, *The Parnas*, pp. 5, 115.

42. Segre, *Memorie di vita ebraica*, p. 229.

Chapter 4. The Moment of Recollection: Turin

1. Attilio Milano, *Storia degli ebrei in Italia* (Turin: Einaudi, 1963), p. 306.

2. Arnaldo Momigliano, "Storie e memorie ebraiche del nostro tempo," *Rivista Storica Italiana*, 92 (no. I, 1980), 194.

3. Primo Levi, *Il sistema periodico* (Turin: Einaudi, 1975), p. 3.

4. Ibid., pp. 5, 8–9, 53.

5. Cecil Roth, *The History of the Jews of Italy* (Philadelphia: Jewish Publication Society of America, 1946), pp. 490, 502.

6. Augusto Segre, *Memorie di vita ebraica: Casale Monferrato – Roma – Gerusalemme, 1918–1960* (Rome: Bonacci, 1979), p. 44.

7. Ibid., pp. 40, 95.

8. Ibid., pp. 87–88. A similar mockery about pigs' ears figures in Primo Levi's *Sistema periodico*, pp. 4–5.

9. Arturo Carlo Jemolo, *Anni di prova* (Vicenza: Neri Pozza, 1969), pp. 51, 53, 56.

10. "Memoirs of David Yona" (mimeographed typescript: Cambridge, Mass., 1971), pp. 11, 71, 206–208. The author anglicized the spelling of his name after his emigration to the United States.

11. Ibid., pp. 69–70, 73–74.

12. Ibid., pp. 88–89, 162, 176–178, 206, 223.

13. On Monti's influence, see James D. Wilkinson, *The Intellectual Resistance in Europe* (Cambridge, Mass.: Harvard University Press, 1981), p. 204.

14. Norberto Bobbio, "Ebrei di ieri e ebrei di oggi di fronte al fascismo," in *La difesa della razza* (special number of the review *Il Ponte*) 34 (November 30 – December 31, 1978), 1314–1315.

15. Carlo Levi, *L'orologio* (Turin: Einaudi, 1950), tr. *The Watch* (New York: Farrar, Straus & Young, 1951), pp. 214–215, "Ricordo di Leone Ginzburg," probably dating from 1963, in Gigliola De Donato, ed., *Coraggio dei miti: Scritti contemporanei, 1922–1974* (Bari: De Donato, 1975), pp. 166–167.

16. Renzo De Felice, *Storia degi ebrei italiani sotto il fascismo*, 3rd ed. (Turin: Einaudi, 1972), pp. 146–147; Luigi Salvatorelli and Giovanni Mira, *Storia d'Italia nel periodo fascista*, 9th ed. (Turin: Einaudi, 1964), pp. 791–792. (Because Salvatorelli knew the group in question, his account is virtually first-hand.)

17. Natalia Ginzburg, *Lessico famigliare* (Turin: Einaudi, 1963),

tr. D. M. Low, *Family Sayings* (New York: Dutton, 1967), pp. 92, 100–111.

18. Natalia Ginzburg, *Mai devi domandarmi* (Milan: Garzanti, 1970), p. 74. This is the second of three collections of her occasional writings, many of them autobiographical, the others being: *Le piccole virtú* (Turin: Einaudi, 1962) and *Vita immaginaria* (Milan: Mondadori, 1974). For the basic facts about her childhood and youth, see Elena Clementelli, *Invito alla lettura di Natalia Ginzburg*, 3rd ed. (Milan: Mursia, 1977), pp. 19–33.

19. Ginzburg, *Vita immaginaria*, p. 152, *Piccole virtú*, pp. 25–26, 92, 97–98, *Mai devi*, pp. 192, 206–207.

20. Ginzburg, *Vita immaginaria*, pp. 22, 25.

21. Natalia Ginzburg, Preface to *Cinque romanzi brevi* (Turin: Einaudi, 1964), pp. 7–8.

22. Ginzburg, *Piccole virtú*, p. 19, *Vita immaginaria*, p. 95.

23. Ginzburg, Preface to *Cinque romanzi*, p. 14. *La strada che va in città* (originally published under a pseudonym in 1942), the first of the five, tr. Frances Frenaye, *The Road to the City* (Garden City, N. Y.: Doubleday, 1949).

24. Ginzburg, *Family Sayings*, pp. 163–165.

25. Ibid., p. 158; Ginzburg, *Piccole virtú*, pp. 18, 88; Preface to *Cinque romanzi*, p. 15.

26. Ginzburg, *Piccole virtú*, p. 69; *Vita immaginaria*, p. 122.

27. Ibid., pp. 119–120; Ginzburg, *Piccole virtú*, p. 22.

28. See her portrait of him in "Lui e io" (1962) in ibid., pp. 53–65.

29. Natalia Ginzburg, *Tutti i nostri ieri* (Turin: Einaudi, 1952), tr. Angus Davidson, *A Light for Fools* (New York: Dutton, 1956), pp. 138–139, 140–141, 160–161, 214. I am at a loss to explain why in this latter title one phrase has been substituted for another from the same speech of Macbeth.

30. Ibid., pp. 28, 38, 57, 96, 192–193, 215, 227, 242.

31. Ginzburg, *Sagittario* (fourth of the *Cinque romanzi*; originally published in 1957), pp. 205, 209–211, 233.

32. Ginzburg, Preface to *Cinque romanzi*, p. 17.

33. Ginzburg, *Le voci della sera* (last of the *Cinque romanzi*; originally published in 1961), tr. D. M. Low, *Voices in the Evening* (New York: Dutton, 1963), pp. 21, 51–52, 95.
34. Ibid., pp. 94, 143, 156.
35. Ginzburg, Preface to *Cinque romanzi*, pp. 17–18.
36. Ginzburg, *Family Sayings*, pp. 5, 31.
37. Ibid., pp. 53, 214.
38. Ibid., pp. 73, 171–172. I have altered the translation.
39. Ibid., pp. 74, 98.
40. Ibid., pp. 18–19, 95.
41. Ibid., p. 135.
42. Two peripheral characters with Jewish names do appear in the short novel *Famiglia* (Turin: Einaudi, 1977); but the author refrains from comment on their origin.
43. Ginzburg, *Mai devi*, pp. 167–168.
44. Giuliano Manacorda, *Vent' anni di pazienza: Saggi sulla letteratura contemporanea italiana* (Florence: La Nuova Italia, 1972), p. 379.

Chapter 5. The Moment of Recollection: Ferrara

1. Jacob Burckhardt, *Die Kultur der Renaissance in Italien* (1860), tr. S. G. C. Middlemore, *The Civilization of the Renaissance in Italy* (New York: Harper & Row, Colophon ed., 1958), I, 67.
2. Dante Della Terza, "Italian Fiction from Pavese to Pratolini, 1950–1960," *Italian Quarterly*, 3 (Fall 1959), 37.
3. Attilio Milano, *Storia degli ebrei in Italia* (Turin: Einaudi, 1963), p. 269.
4. Ibid., pp. 267–268, 299–301; Cecil Roth, *The History of the Jews of Italy* (Philadelphia: Jewish Publication Society of America, 1946), pp. 187–190, 314–315, 320–321; Andrea Balletti, *Gli ebrei e gli Estensi* (1st ed. 1930; Bologna: Forni, 1969), pp. 76–79.
5. Emilio Sereni, *Il capitalismo nelle campagne (1860–1900)* (Turin: Einaudi, 1947), p. 301; Giorgio Porisini, *Bonifiche e agricoltura nella bassa Valle Padana (1860–1915)* (Milan: Banca Com-

merciale Italiana, 1978), p. 32; Paul Corner, *Fascism in Ferrara, 1915–1925* (London: Oxford University Press, 1975), pp. 7–8.

6. Ibid., pp. 124, 128, 170–175.

7. See the account in F. W. Deakin's *The Brutal Friendship: Mussolini, Hitler and the Fall of Italian Fascism* (New York: Harper & Row, 1962), pp. 628–632. In his story based on the incident, "A Night in '43" (fifth of *Five Stories of Ferrara*), Bassani puts it a month later, evidently in order to heighten the dramatic effect with a cover of snow.

8. The words quoted are from "Pagine di un diario ritrovato," entry of February 9, 1944, in the volume of Bassani's miscellaneous prose entitled *Le parole preparate* (Turin: Einaudi, 1966), p. 222. For biographical information, see ibid., pp. 205–207, 223, 236–237; the postscript to the volume of Bassani's poetry entitled *L'alba ai vetri* (Turin: Einaudi, 1963), pp. 85–90; and Massimo Grillandi, *Invito alla lettura di Giorgio Bassani* (Milan: Mursia, 1972), pp. 17–37.

9. Bassani, *Parole preparate*, p. 243.

10. Giorgio Bassani, "Gli anni delle storie," in *L'odore del fieno* (Milan: Mondadori, 1972), p. 142. This essay is missing from the translation by William Weaver, *The Smell of Hay* (New York: Harcourt Brace Jovanovich, 1975).

11. Giuliano Manacorda, *Storia della letteratura italiana contemporanea, 1940–1975*, 4th ed. (Rome: Editori Riuniti, 1977), p. 349.

12. Ignazio Baldelli, "La riscrittura 'totale' di un' opera: da 'Le storie ferraresi' a 'Dentro le mura' di Bassani," *Lettere Italiane*, 26 (April–June 1974), 180–197. A one-volume, definitive edition of the full *Romanzo di Ferrara* (with further revisions throughout) was published by Mondadori in 1980. When I have quoted from translations, I have made sure that the words quoted conform to Bassani's final version.

13. Bassani, Gli anni delle storie," pp 138–141, 143–145.

14. Bassani, "Lida Mantovani," in *Dentro le mura: Romanzo*, p. 33. For the *Five Stories of Ferrara* I am not citing the translation, since it was made from Bassani's earlier version.

15. Bassani, "La passeggiata prima di cena," in *Dentro le mura:*

Romanzo, p. 54.

16. Ibid., pp. 55–56, 62, 64, 66.

17. Ibid., pp. 57–59, 63.

18. Ibid., pp. 59–60, 64.

19. Bassani, "Una lapide in via Mazzini," in *Dentro le mura: Romanzo*, pp. 67–70.

20. Ibid., pp. 81–84.

21. Ibid., pp. 85–86, 96.

22. Bassani, *Parole preparate*, pp. 115, 247, "Gli anni delle storie," p. 146.

23. Bassani, "More News of Bruno Lattes," in *Smell of Hay*, pp. 16, 17; "Gli ultimi anni di Clelia Trotti," in *Dentro le mura: Romanzo*, p. 133.

24. Bassani, "More News of Bruno Lattes, " pp. 28–29, 36–37.

25. Bassani, "Clelia Trotti," pp. 106, 117, 126–128, 133.

26. See Giorgio Romano, "L'elemento ebraico in romanzi di scrittori ebrei italiani," in Daniel Carpi, Attilio Milano, Alexander Rofé, eds., *Scritti in memoria di Leone Carpi* (Milan and Jerusalem: Fondazione Sally Mayer, 1967), p. 200.

27. Giorgio Bassani, *Gli occhiali d'oro* (Turin: Einaudi, 1958), tr. William Weaver, *The Gold-rimmed Eyeglasses* (in same volume as *Smell of Hay*), pp. 162, 168–169.

28. Ibid., pp. 190–193.

29. Giorgio Bassani, *Il giardino dei Finzi-Contini* (Turin: Einaudi, 1962), tr. Isabel Quigly, *The Garden of the Finzi-Continis* (London: Faber and Faber, 1965), pp. 27, 36–38.

30. On the Artom family, see the historical novel by Guido Artom, *I giorni del mondo* (Milan: Longanesi, 1981).

31. Bassani, *Garden of Finzi-Continis*, pp. 40–41, 280.

32. Ibid., pp. 94, 102, 178.

33. Ibid., pp. 23–24, 94, 114–115, 180.

34. Ibid., pp. 73–74, 104, 172–173, 193–194.

35. Ibid., p. 243.

36. Bassani, "Clelia Trotti," p. 123.

37. Bassani, *Garden of Finzi-Continis*, pp. 224–225, 293.

38. Giorgio Bassani, *Dietro la porta* (Turin: Einaudi, 1964), tr. William Weaver, *Behind the Door* (New York: Harcourt Brace Jovanovich, 1972), p. 3.

39. Ibid., p. 149.

40. Giorgio Bassani, *L'airone* (Milan: Mondadori, 1968), tr. William Weaver, *The Heron* (New York: Harcourt, Brace & World, 1970), pp. 6–10, 61.

41. Ibid., pp. 42, 148.

42. Ibid., pp. 80, 87–91.

43. Ibid., pp. 145, 157–159.

44. Ibid., pp. 172, 179.

45. Bassani,"More News of Bruno Lattes," p. 20. The expression *vocazione mortuaria* comes from Cesare Garboli.

46. Bassani, *Heron*, p. 177; Giorgio Romano, "La persecuzione e le deportazioni degli ebrei di Roma e d'Italia nelle opere di scrittori ebrei," in Daniel Carpi, Attilio Milano, Umberto Nahon, eds., *Scritti in memoria di Enzo Sereni* (Milan and Jerusalem: Fondazione Sally Mayer, 1970), p. 336.

47. "Apologue," *Smell of Hay*, p. 68.

48. Natalia Ginzburg, *Vita immaginaria* (Milan: Mondadori, 1974), pp. 177–180. In similar vein, Primo Levi was to declare a decade later, after the Israeli invasion of Lebanon, that it was not to "this Israel" that he was bound by "a deep sentimental tie": "Chi ha coraggio a Gerusalemme?" *La Stampa* (Turin), June 24, 1982.

49. Natalia Ginzburg's *Caro Michele* (Milan: Mondadori, 1973) has been translated by Sheila Cudahy under the outlandish title *No Way* (New York: Harcourt Brace Jovanovich, 1974).

50. Ginzburg, *Vita immaginaria*, p. 178.

Chapter 6. The Meanings of "Survival"

1. Giorgio Bassani, *Il giardino dei Finzi-Contini: Il Romanzo di Ferrara* (Milan: Mondadori, 1980), p. 363.

2. Sergio Della Pergola, *Anatomia dell'ebraismo italiano* (Assisi and Rome: Beniamino Carucci, 1976), pp. 59, 110-111.

3. Augusto Segre, *Memorie di vita ebraica: Casale Monferrato – Roma – Gerusalemme, 1918–1960* (Rome: Bonacci, 1979), pp. 386–387.

4. Antonio Gramsci, *Quaderni del carcere* (edizione critica, Turin: Einaudi, 1975), III, 1800–1801; Arnaldo Momigliano, "Storie e memorie ebraiche del nostro tempo," *Rivista Storica Italiana*, 92 (no. I, 1980), 195.

5. Alfonso M. Di Nola, *Antisemitismo in Italia, 1962–1972* (Florence: Vallecchi, 1973), esp. pp. 12–13, 157–158, 165, 174.

6. Quoted in ibid., p. 57.

7. On this point Della Pergola and Di Nola are in substantial agreement.

8. Michael R. Marrus and Robert O. Paxton, *Vichy France and the Jews* (New York: Basic Books, 1981), pp. 315–321. For a specific case of such protection, see Alberto Cavaglion, *Nella notte straniera: Gli ebrei di S. Martin Vésubie* (Cuneo: L'Arciere, 1981).

9. André Harris and Alain de Sédouy, *Juifs et Français* (Paris: Grasset, 1979), pp. 9, 65, 223.

10. Giorgio Bassani, "La necessità è il velo di Dio," in *L'odore del fieno* (Milan: Mondadori, 1972), tr. William Weaver, "Necessity Is the Veil of God," in *The Smell of Hay* (New York: Harcourt Brace Jovanovich, 1975), p. 7. In the definitive edition of the full *Romanzo* the story has lost its title (as "Gli anni delle storie" has been changed to "Laggiù, in fondo al corridoio") and there are a few textual alterations, one of which, in the passage I have quoted, from "German" to a single synagogue, suggests a stronger stress on universalism.

11. Guido Artom, *I giorni del mondo* (Milan: Longanesi, 1981), p. 108.

12. Ibid., p. 106.

13. Silvano Arieti, *The Parnas* (New York: Basic Books, 1979), p. 85 (author's italics).

14. Quoted in Renzo De Felice, *Storia degli ebrei italiani sotto il fascismo*, 3rd ed. (Turin: Einaudi, 1972), pp. 89–90.

Index